To the Man who loves the Sky.
Dominique—
    We knew that this book had
your name on it. Hope you enjoy
the wonderful moments | dreaming
of Man and the first days of
    Flight.
        John + Elizabeth
            '94

MILESTONES *of* MANNED FLIGHT

MILESTONES of MANNED FLIGHT

The Ages of Flight from the Wright Brothers to Stealth Technology

MIKE SPICK

SMITHMARK

This edition published in 1994 by SMITHMARK Publishers Inc., 16 East 32nd Street, New York, NY 10016.

SMITHMARK books are available for bulk purchase for sales promotion and premium use. For details write or call the manager of special sales, SMITHMARK Publishers Inc., 16 East 32nd Street, New York, NY 10016; (212) 532-6600.

Produced by Salamander Books Ltd
129-137 York Way
London N7 9LG
United Kingdom

CIP data is available for this title

ISBN 0-8317-6050-8

Printed in Italy

10 9 8 7 6 5 4 3 2 1

CREDITS:

Project Editor: Christopher Westhorp
Editor: Philip Jarrett
Designer: John Heritage
Filmset: Bookworm Typesetting, England
Color Reproduction: Scantrans PTE Ltd, Singapore

Front endpaper: *Among the early pioneers of powered flight, the Wright brothers were unusual in that they learned how to control an aircraft in the air beforehand by using a series of gliders. Many of their calculations were initially based on the work of Otto Lilienthal, who made more then 2,000 gliding flights in Germany between 1891 and 1896.*

Page 1: *The Fokker Dr.1 triplane is forever linked with the name of Manfred von Richthofen, the 'Red Baron', top scorer in the First World War and arguably the most famous flyer ever. While not particularly fast, the Dr.1 climbed at a very steep angle, could turn on a dime, and had a rapid rate of roll. These qualities made it an exceptional dogfighter.*

Page 3: *Howard Hughes' HK-1, popularly known as the 'Spruce Goose' because of its largely birch plywood construction, was an eight-engined behemoth with the largest wingspan (320ft/97.53m) of any aircraft ever built. Intended for the transatlantic supply route during the Second World War, it flew just once, making a short hop in Los Angeles harbor in 1947.*

Page 5: *While the airplanes depicted in this book are monuments to the genius of those who designed them, and the craft of those who built them, let us not forget that without the courage, skill and dedication of the men and women who fly them, none of the milestones could have been reached. Inside every machine is a man, like this F/A-18 pilot.*

Back endpaper: *The three great air combat fighters of the USAF form up for the camera over the Nevada Desert. On the left is the McDonnell Douglas F-15, arguably the most capable fighter in service today, while on the right is the small and agile Lockheed F-16. In the center is the ultimate fighter, the Lockheed F-22, which combines supercruise with stealth.*

CONTENTS

FOREWORD

Historians will probably label our current century the era of the development of manned flight. From the pioneering hops at Kitty Hawk in 1903, to the futuristic concepts on today's drawing boards, spans more than 90 thrilling years of aeronautical progress.

As Damon Runyon wrote: 'The race is not always to the swift, nor the battle to the strong — but that's the way to bet.' Many of the early flying heroes risked their lives daily, and a fair percentage paid the ultimate price in the twentieth-century race to further the cause of aeronautics. Civil and military progress during the twenties and thirties focused on engine improvements and the development of airlines and commercial travel. The Second World War developments probably represented the knee of the curve toward higher, faster, longer-ranged and more agile airplanes, all with greater firepower and other military capabilities. The aeronautical race again was survival oriented, with the emphasis on metallurgy, mass production, and amazing leaps in performance.

My flying career started in 1953, and I find that my own experience encompasses nearly half of the 90-year span as a minor participant, and even more as a wide-eyed observer. While being fortunate enough to pilot more than 200 types of flying machines, I have barely scratched the total of types manufactured. As my USMC aviator colleagues are quick to point out, 'There are only two types of aircraft – Fighters and Targets.' At Lockheed, and at General Dynamics before that, we have built and tested more fighters and 'targets' than most manufacturers.

It has been a wonderful, if sometimes heady, experience. Two of us can verify reading well above 940 knots indicated airspeed at less than 500ft in the sturdy F-111. Other, more uncomfortable memories include 9g sustained in flight for 30 seconds-plus in the F-16, three fairly serious crashes, dead stick landings in piston-engined and jet aircraft, a flameout and an airstart in an unusual attitude in a thunderstorm, pylon racing at Reno, MiG flights in Egypt and Pakistan, Paris and Farnborough flight demonstrations, and a dozen aircraft damaged by errant ordnance collisions, aerodynamic panel losses, and a contest with a duck on take-off (we both lost).

Here at Fort Worth we recently celebrated the 20th anniversary of the first YF-16 flight. Several of the guest speakers pointed out that we probably could not develop such a radical new concept in today's world of business development, risk management, product liability and litigation over trivialities. Fortunately, when the time is right, men such as David Lewis, Lyman Josephs and the legendary Kelly Johnson always seem to appear in history. They can see that the future smiles upon the bold. In the F-16, fly-by-wire, relaxed

Above: *Neil Anderson, then General Dynamics Chief Test Pilot, demonstrates the amazing agility of the YF-16 at Le Bourget in 1975.*

static stability, sidestick controllers, the lean-back seat and the one-piece canopy were blended together to present challenges, not obstacles. Recently, the MATV (Multi-Axis Thrust Vectoring) F-16 flew at sustained angles of attack above 80°. Equally impressive statistics are being generated by the family of fly-by-wire airliners that are able to utilize center of gravity adjustments for unprecedented distance flights and marvelous improvements in fuel flows. Fly-by-wire may become as significant in manned aeronautics in space, as well as in atmospheric flight, as was the jet engine in revolutionizing propulsion.

The future is always difficult to predict, but for manned aviation it appears rosy indeed. NASA's triumphs in space may be just beginning, with way stations in earth orbit and permanent bases on the moon or beyond. The F-22, B-2, EF2000, C-17 and 777 all are designed to investigate new and worthwhile technologies for near-term utility. NASP, scram-jet propulsion, hypersonic vehicles, single-stage-to-orbit, and profitable 1,800 m.p.h. commercial airliners could supplement Mike Spick's list in the fine publication which follows.

The excitement of flight continues.

Neil R. Anderson

NEIL R. ANDERSON B.Sc, F.S.E.T.P.

INTRODUCTION

AVIATION TODAY IS TRULY awe-inspiring. Given the money and a modicum of planning, any one of us can girdle the Earth in a matter of days as a fare-paying passenger using scheduled air routes. Alternatively, we can learn to fly and pilot our privately owned or hired aircraft around the country, or even visit other countries. Large airliners carry 500 passengers at a time, while Concorde routinely crosses the Atlantic at twice the speed of sound.

Aviation has shrunk the world in which we live; not in miles, but in time. Journeys which only 100 years ago took may weeks to accomplish are now measured in hours. Peoples on the far side of the globe are now near neighbors.

While this has obvious advantages in terms of transport and trade, it has also had other effects. Warfare has been revolutionized. A single aircraft can carry enough weaponry to devastate an entire city. Others can destroy opponents from scores of miles away, or hunt and kill submarines far below the surface of the sea. Bombers based in the USA can strike at targets in the Middle East and return nonstop. Whole armies can be transported thousands of miles in a matter of days. The implications are enormous. Aggressive nations must now think twice when confronted with air power, which has thus paradoxically become a potent force for peace.

Nor is this all. Aviation has pushed back the frontiers of science and technology to the point where they are barely comprehensible to the layman. Speeds exceeding 2,000 m.p.h. (3,200 km/hr) and altitudes of over 80,000ft (24km) are attainable, and fighters can maneuver hard enough to make the pilot feel he weighs nine times his normal body weight. Clever navigational systems tell pilots

Below: *There is little new in aviation. The latest European fighters all feature canard foreplanes, but so does this Bristol Boxkite of 1910 vintage. Used as a trainer by both the RFC and RNAS, its performance might best be described as sedate.*

where they are to an accuracy of a few meters' distance and a fraction of a second in time. Aircraft can land in visibility so poor that the pilot is virtually blind. Computers can be programed to allow an aircraft to fly at the very edges of its performance envelope without straying into the area of lost control. To quote Ben Rich of Lockheed, 'We could even make the Statue of Liberty fly!'

All this has come about in the space of a mere 90 years: nine decades packed with incident. This book spotlights the significant happenings; the events which led ever onwards; the milestones along the way. Man has long since passed beyond the boundaries of Earth and entered space, but that part of the story must be told elsewhere. Here we are concerned only with the milestones of manned flight.

Manned flight must first be clearly defined, lest we compare cabbages with kings. For our purposes, it is controlled flight in a

powered, heavier-than-air machine. This immediately eliminates gliders (bar those of the Wrights' early work), balloons and airships.

The most difficult task, with limited space available, was selecting the milestones, and inevitably the choice was personal. A few events selected themselves; with others the choice was less clear cut, and many worthy contenders had perforce to be eliminated, although wherever possible these have been given an honorable mention by way of picture captions in relevant sections.

It is intended that the milestones chosen should chart the course of heavier-than-air aviation from its inception to the present day. To present a comprehensive picture it has been necessary to strike a balance among experimental, military, and civilian aviation; between noteworthy 'firsts' and pioneering flights; between human endeavor and technology, and among superlatives: biggest, fastest etc.

The immediate temptation was to select 'first-time events,' but a significant problem was that the majority of these took place very early. As a result, any attempt to use 'firsts' throughout would have inevitably resulted in a chronological imbalance, giving the false impression that little had happened in the last four decades. Another factor is that the theory that leads to a 'first' is often ahead of its time, and many years might pass before technology is sufficiently advanced to make its practical application possible.

For this reason, stealth and several other technologies, notably VTOL and variable geometry, are listed at the chronological point where they reached maturity, rather than when they were first essayed. One classic exception to this is flight refueling, which had all the necessary elements at the outset.

Another area which needed careful consideration was that of records — fastest, highest, biggest, etc. Was there greater merit in the first speed record to exceed 400 m.p.h. (644km/hr) or the first to exceed 1,000 m.p.h. (1,609km/hr)? Bearing in mind the fact that all official speed, climb and altitude records have been dwarfed by an aircraft which could not comply with official regulations, there seemed little point in including them at all. At the same time, absolutes could not be ignored, and the North American X-15, which set speed and altitude records which are unlikely to be exceeded except by dedicated space vehicles, and the gigantic Antonov An-225, which is the world's largest aircraft in every respect except wingspan, are both included.

The first decade of this century saw the birth of true manned aviation when the Wright brothers made their first flights at Kitty Hawk, North Carolina. Before this, several pioneers had succeeded in making short powered hops, but these either used take-off aids such as ramps or the machines were inadequately controlled. The same applied to Paul Cornu's first helicopter flight three years later; it was not the first, but it was the only one to meet the stringent conditions of unassisted controlled flight.

Left: *Sopwith 2F.1 Camels aboard HMS* Furious *in 1918. The carrier variant had a smaller wingspan and, unlike the land-based Camel, was armed with a single Vickers machine gun on the front fuselage and a Lewis gun on the top plane.*

Initially, progress was slow. Not until the latter half of 1908 was real progress observable. Various endurance and distance marks were set, but in the main these were flown over closed circuits, where engine failure would be a disappointment rather than a disaster. It is in this context that Blériot's epic Channel crossing in 1909 must be seen. Both the distance and endurance had frequently been exceeded, but his flight over the open sea, in poor visibility, was a true milestone of manned aviation, and was the forerunner of all trailblazing flights that followed.

By now the military were showing interest in the potential of the aeroplane, and, from 1910 until the end of the First World War in 1918, in innovations. Selecting truly momentous events in this period was far from easy, with dozens of 'firsts' clamoring for attention. Should one include the first aerial reconnaissance, the first bombing raid, the first four-engined bomber, the first air combat victory (Sgt Joseph Frantz and Corporal Louis Quenault, October 5, 1914), or any one of a number of others?

Two events stood out, both of which were to have significant effects on the future of military aviation. The first was the birth of naval aviation, typified by Eugene Ely's ship take-off and landing in 1910/11. (While this was obviously an event of the first magnitude, it could also be followed up by further developments in shipborne aviation, illustrated pictorially.) The second event was the service introduction of the Fokker Eindecker, which was for all practical purposes the world's first fighter aircraft. (This subject also lent itself to a pictorial follow-up of fighter development in the First World War.) As an interesting aside, the Eindecker was also the subject of the first operational experiments in stealth when, in 1916, one or two machines were clad in transparent material in an attempt to reduce their 'visual signature'.

Enormous technical advances had been made during the war. How great these were was quickly shown in the year following the Armistice. On November 27, 1918, a Curtiss NC-1 flying boat took off with no fewer than 51 people aboard, and in the following month an RAF Handley Page O/400 completed the final stages of a flight from England to India. Then, in May 1919, three US Navy NC flying boats set out to cross the Atlantic, staging via Newfoundland and the Azores, although only one made it to Lisbon. Barely three weeks later, in the greatest flight of all, Alcock and Brown made the first nonstop transatlantic crossing in a converted Vickers Vimy, from Newfoundland to Galway in Ireland.

This ushered in an era of long-distance flights, England to Australia and nonstop across the United States, to name but two. While every successful long-distance flight, and many of the unsuccessful ones also, were in many ways remarkable, the ultimate was the first circumnavigation of the globe, or more correctly, the northern hemisphere, by Douglas DWCs of the US Army Air Service,

Right: *John Alcock (left, with camera) and Arthur Whitten Brown used a modified Vickers Vimy long-range bomber, top, when they made the first nonstop crossing of the Atlantic Ocean in 1919, a truly remarkable achievement just 16 years after the Wrights' first powered flights.*

Above: *The Russian Polikarpov I-16 was first flown on November 31, 1933, some 18 months earlier than Germany's Messerschmitt Bf 109, and it entered service in 1935. By 1939 the I-16 Type 17 was the world's most powerfully armed fighter.*

between April 6 and September 28, 1924. Given the reliability of the aircraft at this time, the huge logistics organization set up to support the flight does not detract from it one iota.

Further epic flights followed; a formation flight of six Soviet aircraft from Moscow to Beijing in 1925, England to Australia and back in 1926, and then the flight that caught the imagination of the world – New York to Paris solo by Charles Lindbergh. Kingsford Smith crossed the Pacific from San Francisco to Brisbane in June 1928, staging through Hawaii and Fiji, and Richard Byrd reached the South Pole in November 1929. The first solo circumnavigation was made by Mrs Victor Bruce in a Blackburn Bluebird between September 15, 1930, and February 20, 1931, although the Atlantic and Pacific legs were made by ship. The next circumnavigation was made by Wiley Post and Harold Gatty in the Lockheed Vega *Winnie Mae* between June 23 and July 1, 1931. This flight was of tremendous importance for two reasons. It was completed in a little over eight days, and it had none of the enormous logistic backup needed by the DWCs several years earlier. Just to prove that it was no fluke, Post went around again solo two years later, using the same course but with fewer stages.

Long-distance flying was hazardous, but provided the engine kept running, the fuel lasted out, the pilot stayed awake, and no gross navigational errors were made, it could be done. Rather different was the flight over Everest on April 3, 1933. One of the last unexplored places on the surface of the globe, the Himalayas were notorious for very high winds, rapidly changing weather, icing conditions, and extreme up- and downdraughts. In the event of engine failure there was no possibility of a safe landing.

Meanwhile, other events had been taking place. Cierva flew his Autogiro in Madrid on January 9, 1923, and a few months later the first practical experiment in flight refueling, a technology which, many years later, changed the face of military aviation, occured.

By the mid-1930s war was once again looming. Fighter design had arrived at the monoplane with enclosed cockpit and retractable undercarriage, typified by the Bf 109, first flown in May 1935. (Follow-on pages show other Second World War fighters.) In all fairness it should be said that Russia's I-16 was rather earlier. The same format has been adopted for Second World War bombers, taking the Boeing B-17 as the lead-in.

One other event in 1935 was the first flight of the Douglas DC-3, also known as the C-47 and Dakota. It has few claims to be the first of anything, but its sheer persistence (over 400 remain in service today, and many of these are candidates for re-engining with turboprops) makes it the most enduring aircraft of all time.

For 30 years after Cornu's first flight, helicopter development had languished, but in 1937 the first practical machine, the Focke-

Achgelis Fa 61, was flown in Germany. Two years later, and also in Germany, the first turbojet-powered aircraft took to the skies. This was an event of the first magnitude, as is shown on the follow-up pages of Second World War jets.

Equally important was the development of airborne radar in England. This came to fruition in July 1940, when the first AI-assisted night victory was scored. As in the First World War, technology moved at a breathtaking rate, and it is impossible to do justice to many innovations of the period, such as radar-aided bombing. Just one thing had to be singled out for mention — the ejection seat, which has since saved thousands of lives.

The Second World War saw the first application of carrier-borne air power, a factor which looms large in modern defense considerations. There had to be a turning point here, but which one? The first carrier-versus-carrier battle was Coral Sea, in May 1942. The first decisive carrier battle was Midway, just weeks later. One of the most notorious uses of carrier aircraft was at Pearl Harbor in December 1941, but this was preceded by the crippling of the Italian fleet at Taranto in November 1940, which had actually influenced Japanese thinking. Therefore the watershed in naval aviation had to be Taranto.

Below: *A picture for lovers of mixed formations to savor. No fewer than 22 different aircraft, virtually every major type in the USAF inventory of 1957, is shown here. Within the space of just five decades the aircraft industry, with its diffuse civilian and military strands, had become highly competitive and created a bewildering profusion of different designs to perform a wide range of functions.*

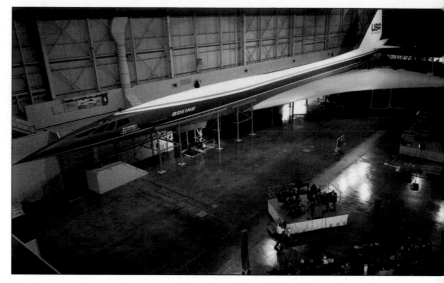

Above: *Dassault's Balzac V was a proof-of-concept aircraft for the supersonic VTOL Mirage V. Powered by a Bristol Orpheus turbojet, it was fitted with eight Rolls-Royce RB.108 lift engines and made its first flight on October 12, 1962.*

Above: *Boeing produced this mock-up of a supersonic transport which was to have been larger and faster than Concorde. Development, however, was halted at an early stage and efforts were concentrated on the 747, which proved to be the correct commercial decision.*

Concentration of force is a cardinal rule of warfare, and the Second World War showed two significant examples of this. The first was the 1,000-bomber raid on Cologne in May 1942, of which one of the participants said, 'This was the first big bomber battle, and the bombers were winning!'. The second was the nuclear attacks on Japan, in which unbelievable force was concentrated in single weapons, with results so dreadful that they have never been used since, though their menace has persisted.

High spots of the immediate post war years were the introduction of swept wings, which changed the shape of almost every high-speed aircraft, and the breaking of the so-called 'sound barrier' by Chuck Yeager in 1947. Other achievements worthy of mention are the development of global reach, notably by the Boeing B-52, first flown in 1952 and still in service in 1994, and the introduction of increasing degrees of automation in fighter aircraft, as typified by the Convair F-106.

On the transport side, the Berlin Airlift demonstrated an unsuspected aspect of air power; that it could be used peacefully to defeat an intransigent, if not overt, enemy. Airliners benefited from the new technology also. The first turboprop airliner flew in July 1948, and the first jet airliner one year later. Both were significant milestones pointing the way to modern air travel.

Technology ran wild in the 1960s. The X-15 attained speeds and altitudes never since equalled, swing-wing technology finally matured and entered service, and the Lockheed SR-71 proved to be an uninterceptable reconnaissance vehicle. Other advances took place in close air support. Before this the helicopter had been very much a utility machine which could carry weapons for certain roles. With the advent of the HueyCobra it took on a new lease of life as a dedicated attack machine which changed the face of the battlefield. Meanwhile, the VTOL or STOVL Harrier entered service, thus fulfilling a long-held dream of a fighting machine that was not

Left: *The huge forward body section of the first Boeing 747 is lowered into position on the assembly line at Seattle to be mated to the nose section. Three body sections were built by Northrop in California and the nose by Boeing in Wichita, Kansas. The nose was then shipped to Seattle for its incorporation in the final assembly.*

dependent on fixed bases. The US Marines' reaction was, 'Great. Park one outside my foxhole!'.

The close of the 1960s saw two innovations on the civil side. The first widebody transport, the Boeing 747, made its maiden flight in February 1969, setting a design trend that all other manufacturers have since followed and revolutionizing air travel at the same time, and one month later it was followed into the air by Concorde, the only successful supersonic transport.

At Le Bourget in 1975 a small fighter piloted by Neil Anderson put on a breathtaking display of agility which made even hardened observers gape in disbelief. It was of course the F-16 Fighting Falcon which, using relaxed stability and fly-by-wire, set standards of maneuverability by which even the latest fighters are still judged. Another standard-setter, first flown in 1979, was the F/A-18 Hornet, which with its glass cockpit and automated displays provided a new benchmark for man-machine symbiosis.

Below: *A tri-jet layout is used by the new McDonnell Douglas MD-11, seen here in prototype form, a design first introduced several decades earlier. The third engine is mounted above the rear fuselage. Innovatory was the use of drag-reducing winglets incorporated into the wingtips.*

The 1980s started on a quieter note. Just one of mankind's many dreams had been to have a limitless source of power, and the sun was an obvious choice. While as yet it does not seem to have brought any practical benefits, the dream came true in November 1980, with the first flight of Solar Challenger.

Meanwhile it seemed that one last challenge remained for the aviation pioneer; to circumnavigate the globe nonstop without refueling. The purpose-designed Voyager was a rather fragile, 'this side up' sort of aeroplane. It was not easy to fly, and its accommodation for the two-person crew was smaller than some dog kennels. This remarkable flight has rightly become one of the great epics of sheer endurance.

The final events were fairly easy to select. The low-speed demonstration of the Airbus A320, the world's first fly-by-wire and 'glass cockpit' airliner, at Farnborough '90, made me hold my breath. The sheer size of the An-225, the world's largest and heaviest aircraft, was equally impressive. The stealthy F-117A or, as our French friends call it, 'le furtif', could not be overlooked as the belated maturation of a very ancient idea, while the Lockheed Advanced Tactical Fighter F-22 will be the trend-setter among fighters for many years to come.

1903
December 17

WRIGHT FLYER

*'Success four flights thursday morning all against twenty one mile wind started
from Level with engine power alone average speed through air
thirty one miles longest 57 [sic] seconds inform Press home Christmas.
Orevelle [sic] Wright.'*

ORVILLE WRIGHT [1]

Thus was an historic moment announced. In previous years, and even days, others had tried. Some had even accomplished short hops, but with these, flying speed was achieved only by taking off down a sloping ramp; with no form of control the man on board was a mere passenger, and flight was not sustained.

By contrast, the first flight by Wilbur Wright at Kitty Hawk was made from level ground, the machine took off under its own power, sustained controlled flight for a short period, then landed at a point at the same height at which it had started. These factors, and in particular the fact that the Flyer was under control at all times, made this the first true powered manned flight by a heavier-than-air machine.

Wilbur and Orville Wright (pictured opposite, top right) were fascinated by flight from their youth. They built their first glider in 1900, and when this was less successful than hoped, embarked on an extensive research program, building among other things, a wind tunnel. Other problems were gradually solved; lateral control in flight using moveable rudder surfaces coupled with wing warping; a suitable lightweight petrol engine, and the precise design of the propellers. Gliding also allowed them to learn to fly before the event; something that most of their predecessors neglected.

Finally, the Wright Flyer (pictured top left, a replica preserved in The Science Museum, London) was ready for the attempt. The brothers flipped a coin to decide who was to make the first trial, and Wilbur won. Few spectators were present; it was very cold and blowing hard as the motor was started. Orville later described the scene:

'With a short dash down the runway [actually a wooden monorail track], the machine lifted into the air and was flying. It was only a flight of twelve seconds, and it was an uncertain, wavy, creeping sort of flight at best; but it was a real flight at last and not a glide.'[2]

The airplane had covered a mere 120ft (36.5m), less than two-thirds of the length of the cabin of a jumbo jet, but it was a start. Then it was Orville's turn. He later recalled:

'...I found the machine pointing upwards and downwards in jerky undulations. This erratic course was due in part to my utter lack of experience in controlling a flying machine and in part to a new system of controls we had adopted, whereby a slight touch accomplished what a hard jerk or tug made necessary in the past. Naturally I overdid everything.'[3]

On the fourth and final flight of the day, Orville remained airborne for 59 seconds (the '57 seconds' cited in the telegraph message was a transcription error) and covered 852ft (260m). From these modest beginnings, the first manned powered flights by a heavier-than-air machine, came aviation as we know it today.

Above, left: *It was not long before the military were assessing the applications of flight and the brothers developed a variant which was tested at Fort Meyer in 1908. By 1909 the US Army had tested it successfully, called it the Military Flyer and set up a school in Maryland where the Wrights could teach America's first pilots. The picture shows one of the Flyers outside its hanger at Fort Sam Houston, Texas.*

Left: *By 1908 the Wrights were referring to their invention as the 'Flyer' and the $30,000 they had received from the US Army had made them wealthy. The brothers took Flyers to Europe during 1908 to demonstrate them to enthusiastic crowds. This image captures the awestruck reaction of French peasants as the promise of the future passes over their traditional present.*

Above: *The Wright Flyer formed a basis for further development. This is the Wright 'R' of 1910. An all-moving horizontal tail surface mounted behind the twin rudders has replaced the canard foreplanes carried on outriggers. The pilot was seated by 1908, rather than lying prone, and extended skids were then fitted to guard against nosing over on landing – a sensible precaution when the engine is located beside the pilot.*

Right: *In 1927 the US Congress authorized the establishment of the Kill Devil Hills Monument National Memorial to commemorate the brothers' historic achievement. Today it is known as the Wright Brothers National Memorial and consists of a 425-acre site covering the area of the first four flights. Atop the hill stands the 60ft (18m) gray, granite Wright Memorial Shaft.*

November 13

STRAIGHT UP

'The way to fly is to go straight up… Such a machine (the helicopter) will never compete with the aeroplane, though it will have specialized uses, and in these it will surpass the aeroplane. The fact that you can land at your front door is the reason you can't carry heavy loads efficiently.'

EMILE BERLINER [4]

A strange contraption sat in the middle of a field near Lisieux, France. Mounted on four flimsy wheels, it consisted of a framework of steel tubes and bracing wires. In the center was an Antoinette aero engine of 24hp, from both ends of which a thicker steel tube projected upwards at about 30°. At each end of this was a large spoked pulley wheel, driven by a belt from a central point above the engine. Projecting from each pulley wheel were two arms with paddle-shaped blades at their extremities. These were the rotors, designed to turn in opposite directions to each other. Below these, on cantilevered frames suspended fore and aft beneath the rotor axes, were control surfaces; moveable planes, the angle of each controlled from levers set on either side of the engine. Uncomfortably close behind the motor was a seat for the pilot, Paul Cornu.

Cornu was a French bicycle maker who, like so many other men of his time, had become fascinated by powered flight. Unlike the Wright brothers, he sought to build a machine that could rise vertically, a helicopter. In 1906 he built his first working model. Powered by a 2hp petrol engine, it weighed only 28lb (12.7kg). It was successful, and he went on to build the full-scale machine, which he completed in August 1907. On September 27, ballasted with a 110lb (50kg) bag of soot, Cornu's helicopter lifted briefly off the ground in an unmanned flight. Further trials followed, until at last Cornu was ready.

The first attempt at manned flight, made on November 9, ended in failure when a drive belt broke. Four days later, on November 13, Cornu squeezed into the pilot's seat, slipped his feet into the stirrups provided, and started the Antoinette engine. Slowly he opened the throttle; the engine revolutions built up, and the rotors turned at ever-increasing speed. With the rotors spinning at 90 revolutions per minute, the contraption shuddered,

then lifted its wheels to about 12in (30cm) above the ground, sustaining this position for about 20 seconds.

That afternoon a further flight was made. At take-off, Cornu's brother was standing on the frame, and failing to dismount in time, he was lifted rapidly to a height of about 5ft (1.5m). Several more flights followed, the longest lasting about 60 seconds, and a forward speed of roughly 7 m.p.h. (11km/hr) was achieved. On some of these a passenger was carried. After this promising beginning, however, Cornu's resources were exhausted, and the project lapsed.

Other French pioneers of the era were the Breguet brothers, Louis and Jacques, and Professor Richet who flew the four-rotor Breguet Richet # 1 (inset, left) on September 29, 1907, at Douai. Seen here in flight, it was stabilized by four men on the ground, making the man on board little more than a passenger. The # 2 (inset, right) was flown with little more success in 1908.

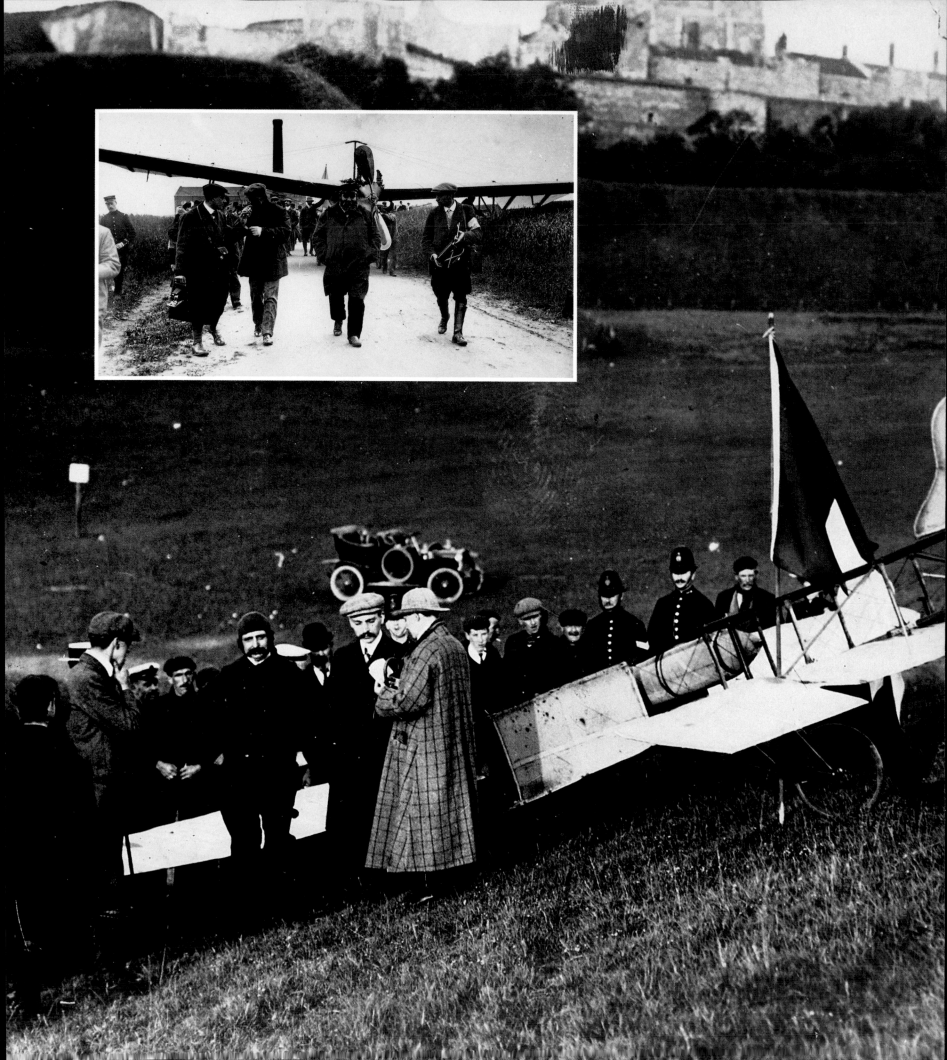

ACROSS THE CHANNEL

'I headed for this white mountain, but was caught in the wind and the mist... I followed the cliff from north to south, but the wind, against which I was fighting, got even stronger. A break in the coast appeared to my right, just before Dover Castle. I was madly happy. I headed for it. I rushed for it. I was above ground!'

LOUIS BLÉRIOT [5]

In 1909 Lord Northcliffe, proprietor of the *Daily Mail* newspaper, offered a prize of £1,000 to the first pilot to fly an aeroplane across the English Channel. During the summer of that year three entrants established bases on the coast of France; Louis Blériot with his Blériot Type XI monoplane at Les Baracques (literally shanties) just south of Calais; Hubert Latham, (inset, second from the left) with an Antoinette monoplane just down the road at Sangatte; and Charles, Comte de Lambert, with a Wright biplane at Wissant, between Caps Blanc-Nez and Gris-Nez.

Latham was the first to try. Taking off in perfect weather at 06.42 on July 19, he coaxed his little Antoinette to the then exceptional altitude of 1,000ft (305m) and set course for Dover, only to suffer an engine failure and ditch just short of half way. He was picked up by his escort, the boat *Harpon,* and returned to Calais, where he immediately ordered another machine.

Within days, all three contenders were ready, waiting only for favorable weather conditions. These duly arrived on the morning of July 25. After a short trial flight, Blériot set off at 04.35, preceded by his escort, the French destroyer *Escopette.* The day was misty, and the English coast invisible. With no compass, Blériot, flying at between 150 and 300ft (45 and 90m), at first steered by following the destroyer, but soon passed her and bored on into the mist. He later recalled the moment:

'For about ten minutes I was on my own, isolated, lost in the middle of the foaming sea, seeing no point on the horizon, perceiving no boat. Also my eyes were fixed on the oil distributor and on the level of fuel consumption. These ten minutes seemed long and, truly, I was happy to glimpse... a grey line which broke away from the sea... It was the English coast.' [6]

A freshening wind had blown Blériot to the north, and he was off St Margaret's Bay. Dover was nowhere in sight, but he could see three boats which appeared to be making for a port. Following their course, he at last saw an opening in the cliffs, where by arrangement waited M Fontaine, a French journalist, waving a Tricolore.

The wind had strengthened, and Blériot (main picture, in flying helmet) was forced to put down where he could, on a downward slope in Northfall Meadow. The landing was heavy, breaking the propeller and both main wheels, but Blériot suffered only minor injuries. The time was 05.12. He had flown 24 miles (36.5km) in 37 minutes.

Just 12 minutes earlier Latham had woken, and, finding conditions favourable he determined also to try, but before he could take off, the wind got up and the attempt was abandoned. He tried again two days later, but once again engine failure forced him to ditch barely half a mile from Dover. The Comte de Lambert, with his Wright biplane, did not attempt the crossing.

Left: *Louis and Mme Blériot at Les Baracques just before the Channel attempt. As seen here, the wings were easily detachable for storage, and the three-cylinder Anzani engine provided a mere 25hp. Following the historic Channel crossing, Bleriot XI monoplanes made many further pioneering flights.*

Right: *The grandson of Louis Blériot, also named Louis, inspects the immaculate Blériot XI at Old Warden, home of the Shuttleworth Collection, where it doubles as both a flying and a static exhibit.*

Below: *One of the oldest aircraft still flying is the Blériot XI of the Shuttleworth Collection, seen here taking off in a cloud of exhaust from the grass field at Old Warden. The same vintage as the aircraft which crossed the Channel, it was built in 1909. It still regularly delights air show visitors on days when the weather is suitable.*

November 14

AIRCRAFT GO TO SEA

'Ely has proved that an aeroplane can leave a ship and return to it, even with crude preparations. Others have demonstrated that an aeroplane can remain in flight for a long time, from five to eight hours or more, that observations can be made from great altitudes, that photographs can be taken, that reconnaissance can be made, that messages can be sent and received by wireless telegraph, that passengers can be carried, that the aeroplane may be stowed on board... and readily assembled for use in less than one hour...'

CAPT W.I. CHAMBERS, USN [7]

US Navy officials were present at Fort Myer in September 1908 when the Wright Model A was first demonstrated to the US Army. They were enthusiastic about the potential of aircraft for naval purposes, but first the problems of ship-board operations had to be overcome.

The task fell to Eugene Ely, a Curtiss demonstration pilot. A wooden flying platform 83ft (25m) long by 28ft (8.5m) wide was rigged over the bow of the light cruiser USS *Birmingham*, and Ely was to have taken off when the ship was steaming at 20kt. But before the ship could gather way, Ely opened the throttle of his Curtiss pusher biplane and rolled forward, off the end of the deck. With insufficient flying speed, the Curtiss dropped toward the water, slowly accelerating as it went (see main picture, left). For a second disaster seemed imminent as it brushed the waves, but the little biplane staggered back into the air, its engine vibrating badly because the propeller had been damaged by

the impact. Seeking safety, Ely headed for the fog-shrouded shore, landing five minutes later on Willoughby Spit, near what is now Naval Air Station Norfolk.

A few weeks later Ely resumed shipboard trials. This time a flying platform 119ft 4in (36.4m) long had been built over the stern of the armored cruiser USS *Pennsylvania*, a much larger ship than *Birmingham*. Primitive arrester gear was provided by a series of ropes weighted with sandbags, which were laid across the flight deck and raised slightly above it by two wooden rails, also intended as guide strips for the aircraft's wheels. Safety rails lined the edges, with canvas nets outboard of these to guard against a mishap.

Taking off from Selfridge Field, California, on January 18, 1911, Ely flew his flimsy Curtiss, now fitted with a spring-loaded hook, out over San Francisco Bay to rendezvous with the cruiser. It had originally been planned that the landing

would be made with the ship under way, but her captain considered that there was insufficient searoom for maneuver, and had anchored.

It was now a matter of precision flying. Too short an approach would result in hitting the stern of the cruiser; too long and Ely might easily overrun and collide with the superstructure. His approach was well judged; he touched down about a third of the way along the weighted ropes, and came to a halt in just 30ft (9m), at precisely 10.01 (see picture overleaf).

After an early lunch on board, Ely took off from the platform, this time without incident, and flew back to Selfridge Field. He had proved that aircraft could be operated from ships, but he was not to enjoy his triumph for long. He was killed in a flying accident later that year.

Henri Fabre's (overleaf) Hydravion had made the first take-off from, and landing on, water on March 28, 1910, but deck landings were deemed preferable for naval operations.

Above, left: *An historic moment as Eugene Ely's Curtiss approaches the stern of USS* Pennsylvania *to make the first ever deck landing. He has to touch down between the two wooden rails seen here, which raise the weighted arrester ropes above the level of the platform.*

Above: *Frenchman Henri Fabre made the first take-off from and landing on water on March 28, 1910, with his Hydravion floatplane, but his flight was just a short hop.*

Left: *Ely prepares to fly his Curtiss pusher off the deck of USS Pennsylvania. The hook for catching the arrester ropes can be seen between his legs. That he did not discount the risks is shown by his padded flying helmet and inflated motorcycle inner tubes around his torso to keep him afloat.*

Above: *Barely an hour after his first deck landing, Ely takes off from USS* Pennsylvania *to return to Selfridge Field. Virtually the entire ship's company turned out to watch him go. Note that the flying platform had a round-down, unlike that on USS* Birmingham, *from which the first ever ship-board take-off was made. From these humble beginnings evolved carrier aviation, which played such a vital part in the Pacific from 1942-45, and the giant supercarriers of today.*

Right: *Short S.27 being hoisted aboard HMS* Hibernia. *It was in this aircraft that Cdr C. R. Samson made the first British flight from a ship under way, on May 2, 1912. Take-off was along the down-sloping ramp seen here. The S.27 was fitted with pontoon floats to land alongside the ship.*

August 1

AGE OF THE FIGHTER

'…my pilot pointed to his left front and above, and looking in the direction he pointed, I saw a long dark brown form fairly streaking across the sky. We could see that it was a German machine, and when it got above and behind our middle machine, it dived on it for all the world like a huge hawk on a hapless sparrow.'

JAMES McCUDDEN [8]

The period known as the 'Fokker scourge' started with the introduction into service of the Fokker Eindecker. A single-seat monoplane with at first one, and then two fixed machine-guns firing through the propeller arc, the Eindecker can be said to have been the first true fighter airplane, and for several months it cut a deadly swathe through its British and French opponents.

The idea of fixed forward firing guns, aimed by pointing the airplane, dated from before the war. These could easily be fitted to an aircraft with a pusher layout, but the aerodynamically more efficient tractor configuration meant that the gun had to be fired through the propeller arc. The problem then became how to fire the gun while not hitting the propeller blades. The answer was synchronization gear which fired the gun when the blades were not in line with the muzzle. This was invented before the war, but technical problems

delayed its entry into service.

A crude solution adopted by Frenchman Roland Garros was to fit steel wedges to the propeller of his Morane Saulnier L to deflect any bullets which might otherwise have hit it. Success came quickly, with four victories in 19 days, but he was then brought down and his aircraft captured. It was examined by Dutch aircraft designer Anthony Fokker, and a synchronization gear developed by Fokker engineers, based on several earlier schemes, was fitted to one of his own designs, the M5K, later to become the E.1 Eindecker.

So far as is known, the first operational flight on an Eindecker was made by Oswald Boelcke (inset top left) on June 24, 1915, and the first combat success was by Leutnant Kurt Wintgens on July 1, although his opponent, a French Morane, came down in the French lines and this victory was unconfirmed. The first confirmed victory came on August 1. It was a

Sunday morning, with low cloud, when B.E.2cs of the Royal Flying Corps raided the German airfield at Douai. Boelcke took off still in his nightshirt, only to have his gun jam. Max Immelmann (inset top right), who had flown the Eindecker for the first time only three days earlier, was more fortunate. Catching up with a B.E. near Vitry, he fired about 60 rounds before his gun jammed. The sole occupant of the British aircraft, Lieutenant Reid, who had left his observer behind in order to carry a bomb load, sustained a bullet in his elbow and was forced to land his airplane on the German side of the lines.

In February 1916 the first British fighters, D.H.2s and F.E.2bs, started to arrive at the front, and from that time the Eindecker's days were numbered. Immelmann was killed in action on June 18, 1916, with his score at 15. Boelcke went on to become the greatest fighter leader of the war before falling on October 28, his final score standing at 40.

Above, left: *The Albatros D.Va was used in large numbers by the Luftstreitkraefte. Slower than the S.E.5a and SPAD XIII, it was also less maneuverable than the Sopwith Camel. The D.Va was flown by the Richthofen brothers, von Schleich, Goering and others.*

Above, right: *The SPAD XIII was the best French fighter of the war. Fast, agile and strong, over 8,000 were built. The ranking Allied ace Réné Fonck flew the Spad XIII, as did the American top-scorer Eddie Rickenbacker, seen here.*

Left: *The S.E.5a was the most famous of all the Royal Aircraft Factory's designs during the First World War, over 5,000 being produced. Very fast for its day, and a stable gun platform, it was used by many of the top-scoring RFC fighter aces. Ball, Mannock, Bishop and McCudden all flew this type.*

Right: *The Fokker Dr.1, although not particularly fast, was very agile and had a high rate of climb. The many German aces who flew it include Werner Voss and Manfred von Richthofen, a reproduction of one of the latter's machines being depicted here.*

June 14-15

ATLANTIC NONSTOP

'Snow was still falling, and the top sides of the plane were covered completely by a crusting of frozen sleet. The sleet embedded itself in the hinges of the ailerons and jammed them, so that for about an hour the machine had scarcely any lateral control. Fortunately the Vimy possesses plenty of inherent lateral stability; and as the rudder controls were never clogged by sleet, we were able to hold to the right direction.'

SIR ARTHUR WHITTEN BROWN [9]

In 1913 the *Daily Mail* offered a prize of £10,000 for the first direct transatlantic crossing by air, but owing to the outbreak of war, there were no attempts to win it until 1919. A west-to-east crossing, utilizing the prevailing winds, offered the best chance of success. Three competitors assembled at St John's in Newfoundland, the nearest start point; the Martinsyde Raymor, flown by Raynham and Morgan; the Sopwith Atlantic, flown by Hawker and Mackenzie-Grieve, and a Vickers Vimy flown by Alcock and Brown, this being the only twin-engined aircraft.

The first away, on May 18, was the Sopwith. The Martinsyde attempted to follow an hour later, but crashed on take-off. Meanwhile, Hawker and Mackenzie-Grieve were plodding eastwards, but two-thirds of the way across a radiator failure forced them to ditch alongside a Danish steamer.

At last the Vimy was ready, and on Saturday June 14, laden with 860gal (1,033 US gal) of petrol, it bumped across the field, scraped over the boundary and vanished into a dip on the far side. Disaster looked imminent, but with both Rolls-Royce Eagle engines at full throttle it finally lumbered into the air.

On a transoceanic flight of this length, provided the engines kept going, navigation was the big problem. The US Navy Curtiss flying boats (inset) which made a staged crossing via the Azores a month before had had 55 warships spaced across the ocean at 50-mile (80km) intervals, marking the course with searchlights and starshells. The Vimy had no such aid, and Brown, the navigator, was forced to rely on 'shooting' the sun or stars with a sextant for position, and taking drift sightings for course variations. Heavy cloud across most of the Atlantic meant that the Vimy had to climb above it to enable the sun and stars to be seen, then descend beneath it for drift sightings to be taken. At one point in the flight Alcock and Brown were at 11,000ft (3,350m); at another they were almost skimming the waves.

The Vimy was not immune from mechanical troubles. The inner exhaust pipe split away from an engine casing, fortunately causing no other damage. The radio and intercom both failed. The air speed indicator froze, giving a constant reading of 90 m.p.h. (145km/hr). This last nearly led to disaster, as the Vimy stalled, dropped a wing, and spiralled down through thick cloud. Just when all looked lost, it emerged into clear air with sufficient height for Alcock to recover control, barely 60ft (18.5m) above the water

Another hazard was icing. Brown several times knelt on fuselage top-decking to chip ice away from the petrol overflow gauge on a center-section strut. At last, with a misfiring starboard engine, they crossed the Irish coast and landed in a bog near Clifden in Galway. They had been airborne for 16 hours 27 minutes, and had covered 1,980 miles (3,186km).

1923
January 9

ROTARY WINGS

'Demonstrated publicly at the Cuatro Vientos airport in Spain, the craft amazed and fascinated the whole aeronautical world. It was safe. Once… it climbed too steeply and lost all its forward motion, which, for the conventional aeroplane, would have meant plummeting to earth. This did not occur.'

COLONEL H.F. GREGORY, USAAF [10]

The rapid development of the airplane following the Wright brothers' first flight was not paraleled by the helicopter. The complexity of the latter, coupled with its inherent propulsive inefficiency, retarded development for many years. But the potential to operate from very small areas and to fly very slowly remained desirable.

To achieve this, Juan de La Cierva attempted to combine the advantages of the rotary wing with the propulsion system of the fixed-wing aircraft in the 'Autogiro'. This differed from the helicopter in that the engine drove a propeller in the nose, and was not connected to the rotor, which was driven by the airflow in forward flight. In Madrid in 1920 he built the Cierva C.1, based on a Deperdussin monoplane fuselage. This was unsuccessful, as were the next two machines.

The main problem was that, as with helicopters, while individual rotor blades gave an equal amount of lift when the machine was hovering, in forward flight the advancing blade created more lift than the retreating blade, thus causing an unstable rolling moment which became worse as forward speed increased. Cierva's solution was ingenious. He semi-articulated the root of each rotor blade, allowing it to flap up and down and also to 'advance and retreat'. The changing angle of attack of each blade thus balanced out the lift around the rotor disc.

Cierva's first successful machine was the C.4. It used a modified Hanriot fuselage with an 80hp Le Rhone engine, and had a four-bladed rotor of 33ft (10m) diameter and stub wings on outriggers both to increase stability and to offload the rotor in forward flight. On January 9, 1923, the C.4 made its first official flight at Cuatro Vientos airport, near Madrid, piloted by Lieutenant Alejandro Gomez Spencer. It covered a circular course of 2½ miles (4km) in 3 minutes 30 seconds, at an altitude of 82ft (25m). Later it demonstrated that it could maneuver freely, and that it could land safely after losing virtually all forward motion. At this stage a moderate take-off run was still needed, but the landing roll was very short. The fixed-wing hazard of stalling on the landing approach had been eliminated.

Further developments followed; the C.6A in May 1924, and the two-seater C.6D on July 29, 1927. Then on September 18, 1928, Cierva, by now based in England, flew across the Channel in his C.8L-III with a passenger aboard. The final development was a system whereby the rotor was initially turned by the engine, then decoupled when flying revolutions were reached, allowing a 'jump-start' to be made.

Cierva C-30As (inset) were license-built by Avro for the RAF, and served from 1934 to 1945 as the Rota Mk1, mainly on radar calibration duties. De La Cierva died in an airliner crash in England in 1936.

1923
June 27

FLIGHT REFUELING

*'One of the vital lessons of our experience over there (the Gulf) was the
vulnerability of tankers. In years past at exercises like Red Flag, our tankers
would orbit outside the exercise area and refuel either side's aircraft as
necessary. Now we are treated as the high-value assets we really are. If we get
shot down, our side loses its fuel supply, and probably loses the war.'*

COL BILL SHERER, USAF [11]

On the morning of June 27, 1923, two de Havilland DH-4B light bombers of the US Army Air Service took off from Rockwell Field near San Diego. One of them, flown by Lts Virgil Hine and Frank Seifert, had been specially modified to become the world's first flight refueling tanker. The modification was crude; an extra fuel tank, a 40ft (12m) length of fuel hose and a piece of rope of the same length.

The receiver aircraft was flown by Capt Lowell Smith, whose idea this was, and Lt John Richter. After flying out to a predesignated area, the two aircraft began edging into position. Gradually the hose was lowered, buffeting in the slipstream, and Smith, coming in from below and astern, maneuvered his DH-4B towards it. Finally he made contact, the hose was inserted into the filler pipe and the fuel was transferred (inset, left). After contact had been broken, the rope was used to haul the hose back aboard the tanker. The first transfer of fuel from one aircraft to another in flight had been successfully accomplished.

The stage was now set for an attempt on the world's endurance record. A 31-mile (50km) course was laid out near Rockwell Field, and on August 27 Smith and Richter once more took to the air. They stayed aloft for 33 hours, 15 minutes and 43.8 seconds, having refueled in flight fifteen times and lapped the course 116 times. The utility of the basic concept was proven.

American interest in air refueling then dwindled, but the British company Flight Refuelling Ltd was founded in 1934 to explore the possibilities. In the summer of 1939 a British air-refueled transatlantic flying boat service began, but was terminated at the outbreak of the Second World War.

Interest was revived after the war, sparked partly by the fuel-guzzling jet engines of the day. Two basic systems entered service in the 1950s; the flying boom used by the United States Air Force, and the probe and drogue adopted by the Royal Air Force and US Navy. The former system can pass fuel faster, and the receptacle on the receiving aircraft is fairly simple. Disadvantages are that a specialist boom operator must be carried, and that only one aircraft can be refueled at a time. The probe-and-drogue system allows up to three aircraft to be refueled at once, but ideally needs a retractable probe on the receiver, and it demands a higher standard of flying accuracy.

Tactical operations in Vietnam were highly dependent on air refueling. Long-range RAF operations in the South Atlantic conflict of 1982 could not have taken place, nor could the Israeli strike against the PLO headquarters in Tunis have been made. In the Gulf War of 1991, air refueling proved indispensable, both for the rapid-deployment phase of Desert Shield and the deep-penetration raids of Desert Storm. Flight refueling has thus given air power a whole new dimension.

April 6-Sept 28

WORLD CIRCUMNAVIGATION

'Midway in Yokohama Bay we passed the volcano O Shima which was putting out great clouds of steam, and soon afterwards thru a rift in the clouds we could see Japan's famous Fujiyama with the sun shining on its snow capped dome some 12,400 feet above sea level — a truly beautiful sight.'

LT LESLIE ARNOLD[12]

Early in 1923 the US Army Air Service became increasingly interested in making a circumnavigation of the globe. Aware that failure would be worse than not making the attempt, the Air Service started planning, virtually on a succeed-at-all-costs basis. The first step was to acquire suitable aircraft, and the choice settled on a Navy torpedo bomber, the Douglas DT-2. Suitably modified, this became the Douglas World Cruiser, or DWC.

A two-seater biplane, the DWC was perhaps an odd choice for a long-distance flight, as it had only one engine. On the other hand it was sturdy and reliable by the standards of the day, pleasant to fly, and the landing gear could be quickly switched from wheels to floats. The DWC differed from the DT-2 mainly in a vastly increased fuel capacity, from 80gal to 644gal (96 to 773 US gal). A new radiator arrangement was adopted, allowing different sizes for different climates, and oak propellers were provided

for the floatplane configuration and walnut propellers for flights with a wheeled undercarriage. Four aircraft, named *Seattle*, *Chicago*, *Boston* and *New Orleans*, were made ready.

The flight started on April 6, 1924, when the four DWCs, fitted with floats, departed Prince Rupert, Seattle, heading for Sitka in Alaska. From here they followed the line of the Aleutians as far as Attu. Already they were one short; *Seattle* crashed in fog in Alaska, although Maj Frederick Martin and Staff Sgt Alva Harvey survived. The next stage involved refueling at sea off Nikolski in Siberia, then on in easy stages down Japan. Crossing to the mainland, they then followed the coast past Hong Kong, Saigon, and Rangoon, before arriving at Calcutta on June 26, where they swapped floats for wheels and changed propellers.

Their course then took the DWCs across the Indian sub-continent to Karachi, on to Baghdad and eventually through into Europe,

calling at Paris and London en route, and arriving at Brough, Yorkshire, on July 17, where they again reverted to floats. Their course now took them northward, to the Orkneys and Faeroes, then on to Reykjavik. It was at this point that *Boston* lost power and alighted on the sea. The thorough American organization paid off; USS *Richmond* was at hand and the crew were saved, although the aircraft was lost.

The two survivors, *Chicago*, flown by Lowell Smith and Leslie Arnold, and *New Orleans*, flown by Erick Nelson and John Harding, carried on via Greenland and Canada, arriving in Boston on September 8, where they swapped their floats for wheels. The transcontinental flight was flown in easy stages, and they arrived back at Seattle on September 28, an elapsed time of 175 days. They had flown a total of 73 legs, over mountains, oceans, freezing ice and baking deserts, covering a total of 26,503 miles (42,405km). It had been an epic journey.

ATLANTIC SOLO

'These phantoms speak with human voices… able to vanish or appear at will, to pass in and out through the walls of the fuselage as though no walls were there… familiar voices, conversing and advising on my flight, discussing problems of my navigation, reassuring me, giving me messages of importance unattainable in ordinary life.'

CHARLES AUGUSTUS LINDBERGH[13]

In 1919, New York hotel owner Raymond Orteig offered a prize of $25,000 (about £5,000 at the then rate of exchange) for the first nonstop flight between New York and Paris. This was a far more formidable undertaking than Alcock and Brown's transatlantic flight in 1919, not least because the distance between New York and Paris was much greater. Reliability thus became a primary requirement, and at that time no suitable aero engine existed.

Progress over the next few years meant that, by 1926, the prize appeared to be within reach. On September 21 that year, French fighter ace Réné Fonck failed to coax his overloaded Sikorsky S-35 trimotor off the ground at Roosevelt Field and crashed, killing two of the four-man crew. Then on April 26, 1927, the Keystone Pathfinder of Noel Davis and Stanton Wooster crashed on take-off with fatal results. The next attempt was made on May 8 that year, when another French fighter ace, Charles Nungesser, and

his copilot Francois Coli took off from Le Bourget in *L'Oiseau Blanc*, a single-engined Levasseur PL.8 biplane. After crossing the French coast north of Le Havre they were never seen again. It began to appear that the task was impossible.

A US Mail pilot, Charles Lindbergh was used to flying at night and in poor weather. His planning for the transatlantic attempt was meticulous. Foremost was the aircraft. He wanted a monoplane for minimum drag, a single engine to minimise fuel consumption (another and rather perverse reason was that with a trimotor there was three times as much to go wrong) and an enclosed cabin. Unlike the other competitors, he proposed to fly alone.

His first choice was a Bellanca, but, unable to acquire one, he turned to the Ryan M-1. Following a downpayment on February 25, 1927, Ryan began building a modified version for the flight. The NYP, as it was called for obvious reasons, was fitted with a 237hp Wright J-5C

Whirlwind radial engine. The wing span was increased, the latest navigational aids were fitted, and fuel capacity was increased to 313gal (376 US gal). To keep the center of gravity within limits, a large fuel tank was fitted in front of the cockpit, completely blocking the windscreen, and the only forward view was through a periscope. The airplane was named *Spirit of St Louis* after the city in which Lindbergh's financial backers were based.

Taking advantage of a brief break in the weather, Lindbergh took off from Roosevelt Field, New York, at 07.54 on May 20. Shortly after 22.00 on the following day, *Spirit of St Louis* touched down at Le Bourget after a flight lasting 33 hours, 30 minutes and 29.8 seconds. He had overcome fog, icing, storms, fatigue and disorientation to get there. Just over two weeks later, Clarence Chamberlin and Charles Levine flew non-stop from New York to Eisleben in Germany. It had been a close-run thing.

Left: *Named* The Spirit of St Louis *after the city of its sponsors, the Ryan monplane was taken on a grand tour after Lindbergh's triumphant return to the United States. Many thousands came to see them and a host of honors were feted upon the pioneer, including the first peacetime Congressional Medal of Honor and the first Distinguished Flying Cross.*

Below: *An endurance flight across a great expanse of ocean was a very dangerous act. Notwithstanding the threat of fatigue there was the possibility – despite altimeters – of disorientation owing to the inability to distinguish between air and sea ahead, running the risk of the pilot flying ever lower and ditching. At one stage Lindbergh was flying no higher than 10ft (3m) above the ocean.*

Left: *Comfort was obviously a consideration for a long-distance journey of such magnitude, as any modern-day transatlantic traveler will quickly appreciate, but Lindbergh's wicker seat was light, strong, and functional, rather than luxurious. It did not, however, impede his capacity for sleep.*

Right: *Charles Lindbergh became a hero figure to a generation of Americans used to seeking their heroes on the sports field. His tickertape parade down Broadway still ranks among the greatest ever. Unfortunately, triumph was to turn to tragedy just a few years later in 1932 when his young son, Charles A. Lindbergh Jr, was kidnapped in Hunterdon, New Jersey, and later found murdered.*

FLIGHT OF *WINNIE MAE*

'With a good railroad to follow, I had no trouble navigating. The only time I can get lost following a railroad is when there are two of them... I rocked the plane when Irkutsk hove into sight. I knew it must be Irkutsk, because we had passed only a few isolated way stations on the line, and I hadn't heard of any other cities in those parts. In fact, I had never heard of Irkutsk until I planned a flight around the world.'

WILEY POST [14]

Wiley Post was the personal pilot of oilman F.C. Hall, whose aircraft, a Lockheed 5C Vega, was named *Winnie Mae* after Hall's daughter, Mrs Fain.

Aviation was Hall's abiding interest and, at a time when he had little need of a personal aircraft, he encouraged Post to look for new uses. Post did not have far to look; his imagination was fired when the airship *Graf Zeppelin* circled the world in 21 days. This was the record that he not only set out to beat, but to halve.

His first need was for a first-class navigator, and the man chosen was Harold Gatty, a Tasmanian who ran a navigation school. Together they began to plan the flight, while the *Winnie Mae* was modified to give greater range, with greatest care being taken to ensure that the trim would not change too much as the fuel was used. Gatty was also part of this operation; he was to shift backwards and forwards as required to balance out the load. Post also

had an armchair fitted for greater comfort for long periods at the controls. Modifications were not confined to the Vega. Post schooled himself in irregular sleep patterns for months before the flight, to increase tolerance to fatigue, as he realized that he would be unable to operate to a fixed schedule.

Shortly after dawn on June 23, 1931, *Winnie Mae* lifted off from Roosevelt Field, New York, and set course for Harbour Grace, Newfoundland. The next stage was the longest, a direct crossing of the North Atlantic to Sealand, near Chester in England. The weather was poor, but they made landfall with little difficulty.

The next stop was Berlin, then on to Moscow, before beginning the long haul across Russia via Novosibirsk, Irkutsk, Blagovesh-chensk and Khabarovsk. The Russians had provided new maps, but these were of limited value only, and Gatty relied on the old navigator's trick of edging constantly

to the left, so that when the time came to search they could turn to the right without having to guess.

Despite bad weather, incidents were few until Irkutsk, where *Winnie Mae* bogged down in the mud on landing. Herculean efforts got her clear, and they took off again after a twelve-hour delay.

From Khabarovsk they crossed to Alaska, landing at Solomon to refuel. Taxying out to take off once more, near-disaster struck when *Winnie Mae* sank in soft sand and bent her propeller tips. The resourceful Post effected a temporary repair with the aid of 'a wrench, a broken-handled hammer and a round stone!' The rest of the flight was uneventful, and they touched down at Roosevelt Field just 8 days, 15 hours and 51 minutes after they had left.

Winnie Mae's adventures were not over. Two years later, flying solo, Post repeated the trip with fewer stops, setting a new record of 7 days 18 hours 49 minutes.

1933
April 3

OVER EVEREST

'Somewhat to my dismay Everest bore that immense snow plume which means a mighty wind tearing across the summit, lifting clouds of powdered snow and driving it with blizzard force eastward. Up went the machine into a sky of indescribable blue till we came on a level with the great peak itself. This astonishing picture of Everest, its plume now gradually lessening, its tremendous southern cliffs flanked by Makalu, was a sight which must remain in the mind all the years of one's life.'

LT COL L.V. STEWART BLACKER [15]

By 1932 aircraft had reached almost every corner of the globe, but one place remained unexplored. Mount Everest, at 29,030ft (8,848m), was not only the world's highest peak; it was located in a remote and inaccessible area of the Himalayas.

Attaining a greater altitude than Everest was not the problem. What was needed was an aircraft with the endurance to reach the area from a base some considerable distance away, and the ability to sustain the necessary altitude plus a significant safety margin for an extended period and operate in the teeth of some of the world's most severe and unpredictable weather. Backing came from Britain's Air Ministry, the Royal Geographical Society, and Lady Houston. The purpose of the flight was twofold; patriotic flag-waving, and a photographic survey.

The airplanes had to be two-seaters with large wing area and room for cameras and other equipment. They had to be capable of being fitted with supercharged Bristol Pegasus radial engines, and to have sufficient ground clearance to allow the use of an oversize propeller. The choice fell on a torpedo bomber, the Westland PV.3, with a Westland Wallace military general-purpose machine as backup. Both were extensively modified.

The base selected was Purnea in India, some 150 miles (241km) south of Everest, which was reached on March 22, 1933. It then became a matter of waiting for favorable conditions. Three de Havilland Moths were in support, and on April 3 one of these reported the mountain peaks clear and wind speed at altitude 57 m.p.h. (92km/hr). This was stronger than desirable, but the PV.3 (by now renamed the Houston Westland), flown by Lord Clydesdale and Lt Col Stewart Blacker, and the Wallace with Flt Lt David McIntyre and cameraman Sidney Bonnet, took off at 08.25.

Not until 19,000ft (5,791m) did they clear the ground haze, to see three brilliant white peaks towering above the clouds; Makalu and Kachenjunga off to the right, and Everest straight ahead, its summit streaming a fierce white plume of snow. On they flew, climbing steadily over huge mountains and glaciers; impossible country for a forced landing.

As they approached Everest a downdraught sent them plunging 2,000ft (610m). Clawing to regain height, they were then swept on an updraught, and at last cleared the summit of the world's highest mountain by the perilously small margin of 500ft (150m).

They circled the summit for 15 minutes in winds gusting up to 120 m.p.h. (193km/hr), with ice from the plume rattling against the wings. Then Bonnet collapsed in his cockpit. This was not surprising; he had earlier trodden on his oxygen feed and repaired it with his handkerchief. The two Westlands now turned for home, touching down after a flight lasting just three hours.

BF 109, LEGENDARY FIGHTER

'I flew only the 109. It was very maneuverable, and it was easy to handle. It speeded up very fast, if you dive a little. And in the acrobatics maneuver, you could spin with the 109, and go very easy out of the spin. The only problems occurred during take-off. We lost a lot of pilots in take-offs. If you were in the air, though, it was very nice to fly.'

ERICH HARTMANN [16]

In 1935 the Messerschmitt Bf 109 was the shape of the future. It was a small cantilever monoplane fighter with fully retractable main landing gear and an enclosed cockpit. Some of these things had been featured on earlier aircraft, but not all together – the only exception being the inferior Polikarpov I-16.

The prototype made its first flight from the company airfield between Augsberg and Haunstten on May 28, 1935, piloted by Hans-Dietrich Knoetzsch. Ironically it was powered by a Rolls-Royce Kestrel engine, as its intended powerplant, the Junkers Jumo 210, was not ready. In timing it was ahead of the British Hawker Hurricane and Supermarine Spitfire.

The first variant to enter service was the Bf 109B, which also served with the *Legion Kondor* in Spain from April 1937. The C and D subtypes followed rapidly, also powered by the Jumo. The latter saw action in the Polish campaign of 1939, but its shortcomings were exposed on November 6, 1939,

when about two dozen Bf 109Ds tangled with nine Armée de l'Air Curtiss Hawk 75s of GC II/4, losing eight for one French fighter.

The solution was already to hand in the shape of the much more powerful and more heavily armed Bf 109E, with a Daimler-Benz DB 601A engine. This, coupled with fuel injection, improved performance enormously, and the E, in various subtypes, was the main German fighter in the Battle of Britain. While speed for speed it could not turn as tightly as its British opponents, in other respects it was superior to them. By employing dive and zoom tactics, the Bf 109 did rather better than hold its own.

As the Second World War progressed, so the Bf 109 was steadily upgraded. The Bf 109E was succeeded by F, G (left) and finally K models. Ever more powerful engines were fitted, and heavier armament, although with the increased weight handling gradually worsened. It was used for a multitude of roles;

interceptor, ground-attack, high-altitude reconnaissance and bomber destroyer. Although in many ways outclassed by the later Focke-Wulf Fw 190, the Bf 109 was numerically the pre-eminent German fighter in all the major theatres of war. Russia, Malta, the Western Desert, Italy; all knew the angular shape and the staccato Thor's Anvil song of the Bf 109.

More Bf 109s of various subtypes were built between 1939 and the end of the war in Europe than any other fighter in history. The total, at roughly 35,000 (records are incomplete), exceeds those of its nearest rivals, the Spitfire/Seafire (22,284) and the Fw 190 (20,001) by a considerable margin.

Almost all the *Luftwaffe* top scorers gained the majority of their victories while flying the Bf 109. Both Erich Hartmann, the greatest ace of all, with 352 victories, and Hans-Joachim Marseille, the top scorer in the Western theater, with 158 victories, flew nothing else.

Left: *The North American P-51 Mustang was the greatest fighter operated by the USAAF during the Second World War. An American airframe powered by a British Rolls-Royce Merlin engine, it was fast, with exceptionally long range. This allowed it to carry the fight to the* Luftwaffe, *escorting the American heavy bombers as far as Berlin in daylight. Although not as agile as the Spitfire IX, it could match the Fw 190A in the turn, while out-turning the Bf 109G with ease. The bubble canopy seen here on this P-51D gave better all-round pilot visibility than either of the German fighters.*

Left: *Old adversaries take to the skies once more as a Supermarine Spitfire and Messerschmitt Bf 109 join up for the camera. They first clashed in the skies over Dunkirk, then, in the fateful summer of 1940, achieved immortality in the Battle of Britain. The Spitfire was the more agile of the two, better in the turn and faster in the roll, while the 109 was slightly faster and climbed better. Both were extensively developed during the course of the war, with the advantage going first to one, then the other. In combat, pilot quality was usually the deciding factor. They remained adversaries even after the war, when Czech-built Avia S.199s (Jumo-powered Bf 109G-14s) flew for Israel against Egyptian Spitfires in the summer of 1948.*

Left: *The most potent German piston-engined fighter of the war was the Focke-Wulf Fw 190, which entered service in September 1941. The aircraft shown here is an Fw 190A-3. While it could not turn with the Spitfire, it had a sparkling rate of roll which enabled it to change direction very quickly. This gave such an advantage in combat that several marks of Spitfire had their wingtips clipped to improve rate of roll at the expense of turning capability. Very heavily armed and armored Fw 190s were used as bomber destroyers, and the type was widely employed in the attack role.*

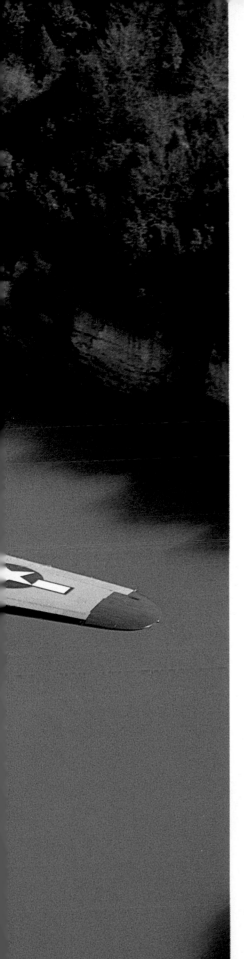

July 17

FLYING FORTRESS

'The Fortress inspired a tremendous confidence. It was the only propeller driven aircraft I have flown that was completely viceless; there were no undesirable flight characteristics. The directional stability was excellent and, properly trimmed, the B-17 could be taken off, landed and banked without change of trim.'

LT JAMES W. JOHNSON, USAAF [17]

With its combination of sleek lines and an inspirational name, the Boeing B-17 Flying Fortress caught the imagination as few other aircraft have, before or since. A four-engined long-range strategic bomber, the B-17 was originally designed to be able to reinforce Alaska, Hawaii or Panama from the continental USA.

Its first flight was made from Seattle on July 28, 1935, with test pilot Leslie Tower at the controls. There is an old saying that if an aircraft looks right, it almost certainly will be right, and so it proved from the outset. Service evaluation of pre-production aircraft took place in 1937, and the first production aircraft (inset) was delivered on June 27, 1939.

Ironically, the combat debut of the B-17 came in RAF service, when three aircraft of 90 Squadron attacked Wilhelmshaven on July 8, 1941. This operation was rather ineffective, as were succeeding raids made at very high altitude, and the experiment was not pursued.

Meanwhile, the Japanese attack on Pearl Harbor on December 6, 1941, brought the USA into the war. B-17Ds were already in the Pacific, and were immediately caught up in the fighting. But it was in Western Europe that the Fortress was to earn undying fame. The USAAF's policy was of accurate bombing in daylight. It was some time before long-range escort fighters became available, and large numbers of heavily armed bombers flew in close formation for mutual protection.

On shallow penetrations losses were acceptable, but for raids deep into Germany the cost was too high. On the other hand, the Fortress gained an excellent reputation for surviving battle damage. Later variants of the B-17 had heavier armament, and the massed defensive guns of the B-17 formations exacted a heavy toll of Luftwaffe fighters.

If the Fortress had one outstanding virtue, it was that it was easy to fly. This was a tremendous advantage because, in the Second

World War, pilots were being turned out on production lines. Although they were well trained, they were young and lacked experience.

The other American four-engined bomber was the Consolidated B-24 Liberator. Designed several years later, it was in many ways a more effective bomber. It was faster and carried a heavier bomb load, but its high wing loading gave rise to some tricky handling characteristics. The slower B-17 was less fatiguing to fly, it was easier to hold in a tight defensive formation, and it could be flown in formation at greater altitudes.

A total of 12,723 B-17s was built between 1939 and 1945, with production tailing off from April 1944 in favor of the B-29. By comparison, 18,188 Liberators were built during this period, nearly half as many again, but despite this the Fortress has the more enduring reputation. The combat swansong of the B-17 came in 1948, when Israeli aircraft bombed targets in Egypt.

Above: *The Heinkel He 111 was the mainstay of the Luftwaffe bomber force in the early years of the Second World War, but lacked performance for the strategic mission. Germany failed to produce a successful strategic bomber. This aircraft is an early model, probably a He 111B of K/88, over Valencia during the Spanish Civil War.*

Right: *The Handley Page Hampden was one of the quartet of modern British twin-engined bombers in service in 1939. Faster and more maneuverable than the larger and heavier Wellington and Whitley, it could not, however, match their payload/range performance, and was withdrawn from front-line service in September 1942.*

Above: *The Consolidated B-24 Liberator was numerically the most important four-engined bomber of the Second World War, with a total production of 18,188 in many variants. A worthy partner to the B-17 in the bombing of Germany, it cruised significantly faster, but was much trickier to handle at altitude.*

Right: *The Short Stirling was the first of RAF Bomber Command's four-engined 'heavies', making its operational debut on February 10, 1941. Very maneuverable for such a big machine, it lacked altitude performance, and was gradually superseded as a front-line bomber by the more capable Halifax and Lancaster.*

December 17

THE IMMORTAL DC-3

'...as you approached Arnhem you got the impression that there wasn't wing-span room between flak bursts, not to mention the small-arms fire! To my right a Dakota, I think flown by Flt Lt Lord, caught fire. Having dropped our load, we banked and weaved as violently as possible to avoid fire from the ground and headed home. ...I never ceased to be amazed at the damage the Dakota could sustain and continue to fly. One came back with a hole in the fuselage large enough to push a chair through.'

FLT LT ALEC BLYTHE[18]

Arguably the most successful and certainly the longest-lived transport aircraft of all time, the Douglas Sleeper Transport, piloted by Carl Cover, made its maiden flight from Clover Field, California, on December 17, 1935. Initially configured to carry 14 passengers in sleeping berths, or 21 seated, in its long career it has carried everything from mules to rolls of newsprint.

The DC-3, as it is better known, was technically advanced for its day. By 1938 it dominated the American domestic market, providing 95% of all scheduled services (inset, left), and by the following year, now used by 30 overseas airlines, the DC-3 accounted for 90% of the world's airline traffic.

The DC-3 was soon adopted by the military, and it quickly became a mainstay of Allied transport squadrons during the Second World War as the C-53 Skytrooper and C-47 Skytrain in US service, and as the Dakota with the RAF. The difference between the two US designations was that, while the C-53 was primarily a troop-carrier, the C-47 was modified to carry heavy freight.

At war, DC-3s carried out many missions apart from basic cargo and troop-carrying. They towed gliders, dropped paratroopers, air-dropped supplies, and flew out the wounded.

The DC-3's list of battle honors is almost endless. It took part in the Allied landings in North Africa in November 1942, the invasion of Sicily, the D-Day landings, the insertion and supply of the Chindits behind Japanese lines in Burma, and flew the notorious 'Hump' supply route between India and China, which involved crossing the Himalayas, often in atrocious weather conditions.

The airborne operation at Arnhem in September 1944, saw C-47s in action (inset, top: US paratroops near Nijmegen). They flew out in neat vics, low enough for the author to see the crews in their cockpits. Later they returned, here a propeller feathered, there holes in wings or tail, cowlings black with oil, often trailing ropes of thick grey smoke, but somehow still flying. Saddest of all was when only two came back where three had gone out.

While only 803 civilian DC-3s were built, military requirements added another 10,123, plus about 2,700 licence-built in the Soviet Union as Lisunov Li-2s. Many flew on the Berlin Airlift of 1948/49.

Even in major air forces the C-47 soldiered on into the 1970s. In USAF service, as the EC-47, it was equipped with sensors for electronic reconnaissance, while the AC-47 was fitted out as a gunship and used in Vietnam in the defense suppression role.

As at early 1994, more than 400 DC-3/C-47s serve with a total of 44 nations. The flight regime is so benign that fatigue is almost unknown, and this has led two companies to offer turboprop conversions, remarkable for a design nearing its 60th birthday.

THE HELICOPTER

*'Professor Focke and his technicians standing below grew ever smaller as I
continued to rise straight up, 50 metres, 75 metres, 100 metres. Then I gently
began to throttle back and the speed of ascent dwindled till I was hovering
motionless in midair. This was intoxicating! I thought of the lark, so light and
small of wing, hovering over the summer fields. Now Man had wrested from
him his lovely secret.'*

HANNA REITSCH[19]

This was the reaction of the famous woman test pilot to her first helicopter flight, in the latter half of 1937. Technical difficulties had delayed development, and it was not until 29 years after Cornu's first flight that a really practical machine was developed.

This was the Focke-Achgelis Fa 61, powered by a 160hp Bramo radial engine. Two shaft-driven rotors were carried on outriggers attached to each side of the fuselage, set to rotate in opposite directions. Lateral and directional control was by means of differential operation of the cyclic pitch to produce asymmetric lift.

The first flight, by test pilot Ewald Rohlfs, took place on June 26, 1937, and lasted just 28 seconds. Gradually the machine was developed, and starting the following year it set a whole series of world records.

On June 25, 1937, it reached 8,002ft (2,439m) altitude, and remained aloft for 1 hour, 20 minutes and 49 seconds. The very

next day it established a distance record of 10.2 miles (16.4km) a closed-circuit distance record of 50.08 miles (80.604km), and a speed in a straight line record of 76.128 m.p.h. (122.553km/hr, 66.13kt). Rohlfs was the pilot in each case.

Hanna Reitsch then entered the record arena on October 25 with a flight of 68 miles (109km) between Bremen and Berlin. In February the following year she made a well-publicized series of flights inside the Deutschlandhalle (inset), although this was not all that well received by the public, who failed to realize the significance of what they were seeing. Two further records were set before the outbreak of war; straight-line distance of 143 miles (230km) on June 20, 1938, and altitude at 11,244ft (3,427m) on January 29, 1939. The pilot in both cases was Karl Bode.

While the Fa 61 demonstrated that the helicopter was at last a practical proposition, it lacked the ability to perform a really useful role. Larger

size and greater power were the answers, and it was followed by the Fa 223 Drache (main picture), first flown in August 1940.

The Drache retained the twin rotors on outriggers, was powered by a 1,000hp Bramo, and had a fully enclosed cabin. Designed for the transport, anti-submarine, rescue and reconnaissance roles, it was ordered in quantity, but only a handful were produced, mainly owing to Allied bombing.

In September 1945 a lone Drache was flown across the English Channel for evaluation, its German crew accompanied by RAF personnel, but it was destroyed in an accident the following month.

The twin-rotor configuration of the Focke-Achgelis design was unwieldy, and American pioneers Bell and Sikorsky used the 'penny-farthing' layout in their Model 30 and VS-300 machines, as did the Sikorsky R-4, which was used on operational trials in the final months of the war.

Right: *The Vought Sikorsky VS 300 made its first successful tethered flight on September 14, 1939. Not until May of the following year did it first fly free. Very much a proof-of-concept machine, it had two horizontal tail rotors on outriggers, but was modified later to have a single vertical tail rotor.*

Below: Genevieve, *the Bell Model 30, is seen here in 1943, flown by test pilot Floyd Carlson. A workmanlike machine, the Model 30 was a pioneer of the 'penny-farthing' configuration for helicopters, in which a vertical tail rotor was used to counter engine torque. Also new was the twin-bladed teetering-head rotor, which became a feature of Bell helicopters for many years.*

Above: *American servicemen crowd around a Sikorsky R-4 for what is probably their first sight of a helicopter. Given the company designation VS 316, the R-4 was designed as a two-seater, able to carry a useful load of 549lb (250kg). First flown in January 1942, the prototype went on to set several new helicopter records, and was adopted by the US Army. The R-4 was the first helicopter to see large-scale military service.*

Left: *Fitted with inflatable 'boots', the R-4 could operate from water, snow or mud, or from the deck of a ship. The first ship-borne trials were held aboard the tanker* Bunker Hill *in May 1943, and later that year it was flown with a canvas stretcher container for the medical evacuation role. It was operated by the US Navy as the HNS, and by the RAF and RN as the Hoverfly I.*

JET AGE!

'For the first time I was flying by jet propulsion. No engine vibrations. No torque and no lashing sound of the propeller. Accompanied by a whistling sound, my jet shot through the air. Later when asked what it felt like, I said, "It felt as though angels were pushing".'

GENERALLEUTNANT ADOLF GALLAND [20]

The Heinkel He 178 was a small and fairly basic aircraft (inset, top left). What made it exceptional was that it was powered by a gas turbine, or jet engine. Work on this type of propulsion was in hand in other countries, but Germany had reached the starting line first. Now, at 06.00 on Sunday, August 27, 1939, Flugkapitan Erich Warsitz opened the throttle and sent the strange-looking propellerless machine trundling down the runway at Marienehe. Gradually it gained speed, and after a rather long run, lifted into the air.

The landing gear was locked down, and no attempt was made to explore the flight envelope. It was enough to prove the new propulsion system. Warsitz turned back towards the airfield, but mist was rolling in, and he had to fly several circuits before it was clear enough to land. This first flight by jet propulsion lasted 15 minutes.

Ernst Heinkel's next jet was the He 280, the world's first jet fighter.

Piloted by Fritz Schaefer, this duly flew on March 30, 1940 (inset, top right). Although it showed considerable promise, official reactions were cool, and no orders were placed.

Rival Willi Messerschmitt had better luck with his Me 262, which made its first turbojet-only flight on July 18, 1942. This was ordered into service, and 13 evaluation models were delivered in March and April 1944. The Me 262 (left) had an outstanding performance for its day, with a top speed of 540 m.p.h. (869km/hr) and the ability to reach 30,000ft (9,144m) in seven minutes. It became operational with *Kommando Nowotny* in September 1944.

It has often been suggested that large numbers of Me 262s could have turned the tide of the war in 1944/45. This seems unlikely. While the performance of the Me 262 was exceptional, it was bedevilled throughout its service career by unreliable engines. The fact was that

German propulsion technology had outrun metallurgical capability.

Quite apart from unreliable engines, the Me 262 had several operational shortcomings. Acceleration was poor, endurance was short, and if it could be caught low and slow on its landing approach, or shortly after take off, it was vulnerable. This weakness was exploited by Allied fighter pilots, who loitered by the approaches to known Me 262 airfields.

The only other German jet to become operational was the Arado Ar 234 Blitz light bomber, first flown on June 15, 1943. As a bomber it was not terribly effective, but at operational speeds and altitudes it was virtually uninterceptable, and it carried out some very valuable high-level reconnaissance missions.

The only Allied jet aircraft to enter service during the war was the Gloster Meteor I, which made its first war sortie on August 4, 1944. Me 262s and Meteors were fated never to meet in the air.

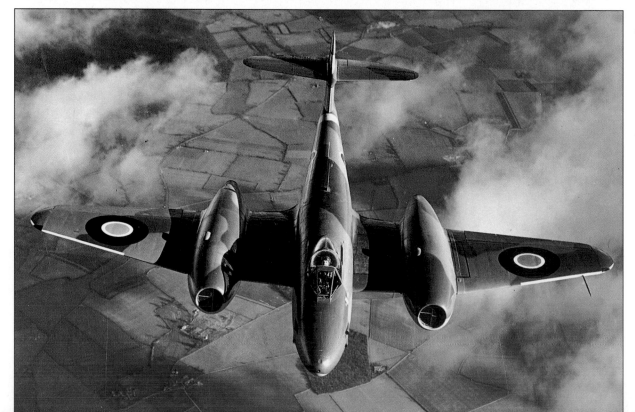

Above, left: *The Messerschmitt Me 163 was the only rocket-powered fighter to see action. Its high rate of climb enabled take-off to be delayed until the last moment, which was necessary as its endurance was very short. Its mix of unstable liquid fuels made it almost as dangerous to its pilots as it was to the enemy.*

Above, right: *Originally designed as a reconnaissance aircraft, the Arado Ar 234 was the only jet bomber to enter service during the Second World War. At high altitudes it was so fast as to be almost uninterceptable. Take-off was from a wheeled trolley, landing being made on a retractable skid. This arrangement posed severe ground handling problems.*

Center: *The Gloster E.28/39 was the first British jet. A purely experimental type, powered by a Whittle W.1 turbojet giving 860lb (390kg) thrust, it first flew at Cranwell on May 15, 1941.*

Left: *The Gloster Meteor became operational in July 1944. Successful against Doodlebugs, it never encountered the Me 262 in the air. The example seen here is a Meteor Mk III.*

Right: *The Bell XP-59A was the first American jet fighter, and first flew on October 1, 1942. Badly underpowered and lacking performance, it was soon eclipsed by the far superior Lockheed P-80 Shooting Star, and saw only very limited service.*

Below: *A deck-load of captured German aircraft is ferried back to the USA after the war for testing and evaluation. Two Me 262s are nearest the camera.*

VICTORY AT NIGHT

'Instructions from Sticks became more and more rapid… "He is about 10 degrees above and dead ahead at about 200 yards". I adjusted my gunsight and searched for tell-tale exhaust flickers or a black object blotting out the stars. One second there was nothing, then, as if from nowhere, it was there.'

WG CDR J.R.D. BRAHAM, DSO DFC AFC [21]

The task of the night fighter in the early days of the Second World War was once pithily described as like being in the Albert Hall on a dark night with the lights out, looking for a black cat that was not there! One thing was certain; throughout the First World War and in the early years of the Second, night bomber losses to operational attrition far exceeded those caused by enemy fighter action. The problem was that ground radar was not accurate enough to place a fighter within visual distance of a bomber. Only when a radar set was developed that was small enough to be carried in a fighter did any prospect of countering night raiders emerge. Even then the execution was far from easy.

The problem with radar was that, even when it worked properly, it showed the operator only where the target was at any given moment in relation to the fighter. From a succession of contacts, the operator then had to deduce what the target

was doing, and guide his pilot into an attacking position.

Airborne interception radar, or AI, was still in its early development stages in the first nine months of 1940. Practice interceptions with scientists handling the equipment gave promising results, but in the hands of the squadrons it was not so good. The 'magic mirror' was initially held in low esteem. A victory at night was badly needed.

At 23.00 on the night of July 22, 1940, Fg Off G. 'Jumbo' Ashfield took off from Tangmere on the Sussex coast. Patrolling over base at 10,000ft (3,050m), he was informed that a small group of bombers was crossing out near Selsey at 6,000ft (1,830m). Turning toward them, he launched into a gentle dive to increase speed. His Bristol Blenheim (left) had little speed advantage over lightly laden homeward-bound bombers.

Peering into his twin scopes, radar operator Sgt Leyland finally gained a contact at about 5,000ft (1.5km)

range, and the observer, Plt Off Morris, caught a brief glimpse of the enemy aircraft as it crossed ahead from left to right and slightly higher. Slowly, Leyland guided his pilot in behind it, until Ashfield was able to see it outlined against the moon. It was a Dornier Do 17 of 2/KG 3. Closing to about 400ft (122m), Ashfield opened fire.

Hit, the Dornier lurched to the left, but as Ashfield tried to follow he was struck by debris from his victim, and his cockpit became covered in thick oil. Breaking off the action, he found that he was inverted at low level. The Dornier had vanished, but shortly afterwards the British flyers observed a blaze on the surface of the sea a few miles off the coast. It marked the bomber's final resting place.

Ashfield's success was a turning point in air warfare. Night and poor weather were no longer protection for the bomber. Within 25 years a fighter without radar had become unthinkable.

Left: *The first aircraft designed as a radar-equipped night fighter was the Northrop P-61 Black Widow. All previous night fighters had been modified or were derived from other types, such as the Blenheim If in the leading picture, developed from a light bomber. Designed to meet all eventualities, the Black Widow was large, cumbersome, and took a long time to enter service.*

Right, top: *Modified from a light bomber, the de Havilland Mosquito was the most effective night fighter of the Second World War. Fast and agile, it ranged the length and breadth of Europe seeking out German night fighters. This is the NF Mk 2, with dipole aerials on the nose and beneath the wings. Later models had a radar scanner in the nose.*

Right, center: *Also developed from a bomber was the German Junkers Ju 88G night fighter. This model, captured and in British markings, carries Lichtenstein SN-2 radar, which works on a relatively long wavelength. This gives rise to the huge 'toasting fork' nose aerial array, supplemented by further aerials beneath the wings.*

Right, bottom: *The Messerschmitt Bf 110 was designed as a long-range heavy fighter, but proved a failure in daylight against enemy fighters. Adapted for night operations it became the mainstay of the Luftwaffe night fighter force for much of the war, although towards the end it was so loaded with equipment that its performance suffered badly.*

TARANTO

'Into that inferno, two waves of Swordfish danced a weaving arabesque of death and destruction with their torpedoes, flying into the harbour only a few feet above sea level — so low that one or two of them actually touched the water with their wheels. Nine other spidery biplanes dropped out of the night sky, appearing in a crescendo of noise in vertical dives from the slow-moving glitter of parachute flares.'

CDR CHARLES LAMB [22]

Traditionally, the projection of power at a distance had been the province of navies, using their primary weapon, the battleship. The advent of the airplane had cast doubts on the validity of this, but the thesis was far from proven. The first year of the Second World War saw extensive use of carrier-borne aircraft, mainly against shore targets.

In 1940 the Italian Navy possessed the strongest force in the Mediterranean. It consisted of six battleships, five cruisers and twenty destroyers. Notwithstanding this, it could rarely be tempted out of harbor and into a position where a fleet action might ensue, but its very presence posed a significant threat to British naval operations in the Mediterranean area.

The alternative was to strike it in its lair. Plans for this had initially been drawn up in 1938, when war seemed inevitable. But Taranto harbor was a tough nut to crack. It had an inner and an outer harbor, defended by hundreds of guns and a balloon barrage, while the capital ships were well protected by anti-torpedo nets.

Two aircraft carriers were available, but HMS *Eagle* developed problems which caused her to be withdrawn. A few of her aircraft were transferred to HMS *Illustrious* for the attack, which was set for November 11, 1940. The attacking aircraft were Fairey Swordfish, slow biplanes which would not have looked out of place in the First World War. Far too vulnerable in daylight, they would have to attack under cover of darkness.

The first wave of 12 aircraft set off at 20.57 from a position 170 miles (274km) southeast of Taranto. Six carried torpedoes, four carried bombs, and the other two had bombs and flares. The second wave of nine aircraft took off 26 minutes later, five armed with torpedoes, two with bombs and two with flares and bombs. A mechanical fault caused one to return early; the rest pressed on.

Charles Lamb carried flares and bombs in the first wave. Unable to see any hits through the storm of tracer from the defending guns, he asked his observer, only to be told, 'No. You were throwing the aircraft about like a madman, and every time I tried to look over the side, the slipstream nearly tore off my goggles!' He slowly became convinced that few, if any, Swordfish could have survived.

In fact, only two Swordfish went down, and the crew of one of these were taken prisoner. The attack was a tremendous success. One battleship sank in shallow water, while two more and two heavy cruisers were badly damaged. The Italian fleet played little further part in the war.

Taranto clearly demonstrated the capital ship's vulnerability to air attack, a fact that was underlined a year later by the Japanese attack on the US Pacific Fleet at Pearl Harbor, followed by the huge carrier battles of the Pacific War.

1,000 OVER COLOGNE

'Against this pale, duck-egg blue and greyish mauve were silhouetted a number of small black shapes: all of them bombers, and all of them moving the same way. One hundred and thirty-four miles ahead, and directly in their path, stretched a crimson-red glow; Cologne was on fire. Already, only twenty-three minutes after the attack had started, Cologne was ablaze from end to end, and the main force of the attack was still to come.'

GP CAPT LEONARD CHESHIRE, VC, DSO[23]

The 1,000-bomber raid on Cologne at the end of May 1942 was a turning point in the air war. Daylight raids were too costly, and the RAF bombing offensive had long since switched to the cover of night for strategic operations.

At this stage of the war, RAF Bomber Command was the only force able to carry the fight to the heart of the German homeland, but results were poor. Only one crew in every five managed to place their bombs within five miles (8km) of the target; and only one in ten did so in the Ruhr, where haze made target location even more difficult.

In 1942 bombers were urgently needed to reinforce Coastal Command against the U-boat menace, and also to interdict Rommel's supply lines to the desert. With operations over Germany demonstrably ineffective, the whole future of Bomber Command was in doubt. Then, on February 22, Air Marshal Harris assumed command.

What was needed was a success, something to show that the bombers could achieve worthwhile results. A really big raid was the answer. The Luftwaffe had put 500 sorties over London on a single night during the Blitz; double this number, a nice round figure of 1,000, would be the answer.

Three main problems had first to be solved. Scraping together 1,000 bombers was a mammoth task, and was achieved only by using aircraft and crews from training units. This was a tremendous risk, as it jeopardized the whole future of the force if things went wrong.

Concentration of force was next. On previous raids bombers had roamed the sky haphazardly, each aircraft responsible for finding and bombing its own target. This was not good enough; Harris wanted to put the entire force over the target in the space of one hour, a bomber every 3.5 seconds. This was too great a collision risk, and the time was extended to 90 minutes. Using

three aiming points also helped to space the bombers more widely. Good timing was essential; seven different types of bomber, each with its own cruising speed and altitude, were to be used. Finally, the target had to be easy to find, even in less-than-perfect conditions. Cologne, marked by the river Rhine, was eventually chosen.

On the night of May 30 no fewer than 1,046 bombers set out over the North Sea. Bringing up the rear were 67 of the new and fast Lancasters (main picture, with bomb bay inset). All converged on a point off the Dutch coast, from where they headed directly for the target. The German night fighter defenses were swamped by the concentrated bomber stream; for each bomber intercepted dozens passed through unscathed.

In all, 48 bombers were lost that night; an acceptable level of attrition. Cologne was devastated. This was the beginning of the road back for Bomber Command.

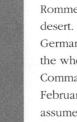

EJECTION!

'I got the kick up the backside as my seat fired. I heard or sensed each action in turn: the cartridges firing in my seat, my drogue gun going, and my seat tumbling as I left the aircraft. I was fully conscious, and I remember thinking, when are all these explosions going to stop? Then suddenly there was a dead silence, absolutely no noise at all, and I was hanging from my parachute.'

FLT LT RUPERT CLARK, RAF [24]

The incident described above took place on February 14, 1991, when Flt Lt Clark's Tornado GR.1 was shot down by an Iraqi surface-to-air missile. At the time of writing, between ten and fifteen thousand aircrew owe their lives to the ejection seat, which must therefore rank as one of the most important inventions in military aviation.

Although the parachute had been successfully used in 1797, not until the summer of 1918 was it used to save airmen from crashing or burning aircraft. Its use soon became widespread, but as aircraft speeds increased during the 1930s and 1940s, getting clear of the machine became increasingly difficult. Even when this was possible, serious injury could be caused if the escapee was hit by the tail surfaces. A German report of the era showed that two in every five emergency escapes resulted in fatalities. What was needed was a device to throw the pilot or crewman clear.

The first ejection seat was German, using compressed air propulsion. Fitted in the Heinkel He 280 jet fighter, it was first flown on April 2, 1941.

The He 280 did not enter service, and the prototype was fitted with four Argus pulse jets. On January 13, 1943, this aircraft was towed into the air for testing, but at 7,875ft (2,400m) Argus test pilot Schenk found that he was unable to jettison the towline. Faced with the prospect of landing with the towline in place, he wisely decided to abandon the aircraft, thus becoming the first man to eject successfully from an aircraft in flight.

The first aircraft to become operational with an ejection seat fitted was the Heinkel He 219 night fighter. While the performance of the seat was marginal, 60 lives are believed to have been saved by it.

The second operational fighter fitted with an ejection seat was Saab's J.21A, a pusher aircraft with twin tailbooms, first flown in 1943. An explosive charge was used to lift the pilot clear of the pusher propeller.

The advent of jet aircraft made the provision of ejector seats vital, and Britain and the USA started work on them in the final years of the Second World War. On July 24, 1946, Bernard Lynch of Martin-Baker ejected from a Meteor III in the first fully documented trial (inset). Face blinds and arm and leg restraints followed as the problems became known.

One of these was escape velocity. The human frame could stand only so much, and acceleration had to be limited, even though a high trajectory was needed. Using rockets, rather than explosive charges, to provide motive power kept the acceleration within the limits.

Today we have zero altitude/zero speed seats (main picture shows the Stencel S III-S3) which enable the crew to get clear if, for example, the aircraft catches fire on the ground; and seats which seek the correct attitude, enabling escapes to be made at almost any angle.

August 6

HIROSHIMA

'A column of smoke rising fast. It has a fiery red core. A bubbling mass, purple-grey in colour, with that red core. It's all turbulent. Fires are springing up everywhere, like flames shooting out of a huge bed of coals... Here it comes, the mushroom shape... It's coming this way. It's like a mass of bubbling molasses. The mushroom is spreading out. It's maybe a mile or two wide and half a mile high. It's growing up and up and up... The base of the mushroom looks like a heavy undercast that is shot through with flames.'

TECH SGT GEORGE CARON [25]

At 02.42 on the morning of August 6, 1945, the huge Boeing B-29 Superfortress was cleared for take-off from the island of Tinian in the Marianas. At the controls was Col Paul Warfield Tibbets (inset left, at center with crew), a man carefully selected and trained to carry out the most destructive bombing mission ever. In the bomb bay was Little Boy, the first atomic bomb.

Little Boy (inset, right), a Uranium 235-based weapon, was the culmination of the Manhattan Project, a nuclear research program lasting many years and costing many billions of dollars. Along with Fat Man, its plutonium-based companion, later to be dropped on Nagasaki, it was to be used to bring the war in the Pacific to a quick end.

The flight engineer opened the throttles, and slowly the B-29 started to move down the runway. For those in the know, this was a fraught time. A crash on take-off could possibly cause premature detonation, which would wipe out the whole of Tinian.

The B-29 was overloaded, and Tibbets held it on the ground until the very last moment before easing back on the yoke. Slowly the huge bomber, named *Enola Gay* after Tibbets' mother, left the runway and climbed away into the darkness. On board, the navigator, radar operator and radioman were busy checking the course. Nothing could be left to chance. Ahead lay the target, Hiroshima.

Enola Gay arrived over Iwo Jima as dawn broke, and the pilot set course for Shikoku, climbing to bombing altitude of 30,600ft (9,325m) as it neared the Japanese coast. Ahead, a weather reconnaissance B-29 had reached Hiroshima and reported conditions satisfactory. The die was cast.

At 08.14, Tibbets gave the command 'On glasses,' and the crew donned heavy Polaroid goggles to protect their eyes from the flash. Bombardier Maj Thomas Ferebee lined up the aiming point, the Aioi bridge in the middle of the city, and at 08.15.17 Little Boy fell clear.

Tibbets instantly swung *Enola Gay* into a hard, diving right-hand turn through 155°, away from the detonation. They had less than a minute to make good their escape from the blast. No-one knew whether this would be enough; they could only hope.

At precisely 08.16 the bomb detonated with a force equal to 20,000 tons of TNT, and a glare far brighter than the sun. Tibbets could '... taste the brilliance; it tasted like lead.' On the ground a firestorm raged, and radiation, the quiet, insidious killer, passed unnoticed through walls and bodies. Some 71,379 people died, 68,000 were injured, and 49,000 buildings were destroyed. Above, the mile-wide mushroom cloud rose to 60,000ft (18km), marking the place where a city called Hiroshima had been. The nuclear age was born, and the world would never be the same again.

October 1

SWEPT WINGS

'I've been followed by a MiG from 27,000ft (8,229m) to 5,000ft (1,524m), pulling maximum "Gs" at high speed. So violent were the turns that both my oxygen mask and flying helmet slipped. In following me down the MiG was, however, unable to hit me as he could not get enough deflection — although he appeared to use all his ammunition in trying to do so.'

SQN LDR W 'PADDY' HARBISON RAF, CFE [26]

The advent of the jet engine made transonic speeds possible, but these were accompanied by a large drag rise. However, it was found that this could be delayed by sweeping the wings at an angle of 35° or more. This effectively reduced the velocity of the airflow and with it the drag, by a factor of the cosine of the sweep angle. This knowledge was put to good use in the design of two of the greatest fighters of the early 1950s, the F-86 Sabre (left) and the MiG-15 (inset).

The Sabre first flew on October 1, 1947, and the MiG-15 three months later, on December 30. They were both swept-wing, single-engined single-seaters. The Russian jet was the smaller of the two; it was also considerably lighter. Whereas the Sabre was a very sophisticated fighter for its day, the MiG-15 was basic. The American fighter was armed with six 0.50-caliber machine guns, whereas the MiG carried two 23mm and one 37mm cannon. Their

engines were of comparable power, the F-86 having a General Electric J47, and the MiG an RD 45 based on the British Rolls-Royce Nene.

The Russian fighter possessed far superior high-altitude and climb performance, but the American aircraft had incomparably better handling qualities. It could also exceed Mach 1 in a dive, which it did for the first time on April 26, 1948, whereas the MiG-15 was firmly subsonic. Both were for years the mainstays of their respective countries' air defenses, and were widely exported.

The war in Korea saw them clash. The first engagement came on December 17, 1950, exactly 48 years after the Wright brothers' historic flight, when Lt Col Bruce Hinton of the 336th Fighter Sqn shot down a MiG-15. It was the first of many.

The period for which full data is available runs from July 1951 to the end of the war, in July 1953. During this period, F-86s accounted for 757 MiGs while suffering 103 losses, a

ratio of slightly less than 7.5:1, achieved while operating at an average force advantage, measured in sorties flown, of just under 2:1. This was a remarkable achievement, in view of the fact that altitude had traditionally been held to be the greatest advantage in air combat, and the MiG-15 had by far the better altitude performance of the two, with the added advantage of ground radar coverage of much of the area.

Why, then, did the Sabre emerge the victor by such a clear margin? Basically because it was the better fighter of the two. It combined superb handling qualities with a radar ranging gunsight which, although often temperamental, gave very accurate aiming. Its ability to remain under full control at very high Mach numbers was not matched by its Russian opponent. These factors allowed the USA to establish a qualitative superiority over Soviet products, a technical lead which was never lost during the decades of the Cold War.

Left: *The Grumman Cougar is of particular interest in that it was essentially a straight-wing F9F Panther with 35° swept wings and tail surfaces grafted on to delay the transonic drag rise. Spoilers were used instead of ailerons, with wing fences to minimize spanwise flow. The aircraft depicted is an F9F-8P.*

Below, left: *Although similar in appearance to the MiG-15, the MiG-17 was extensively redesigned to overcome the worst features of the earlier aircraft. Spanwise flow was a problem with swept wings, and the MiG-17 had three large fences to correct this, which did nothing to reduce drag. It was, however, a very pleasant aircraft to fly.*

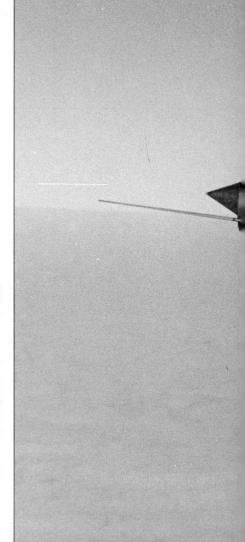

Right: *A delta wing, as used by the Dassault Mirage IIID seen here, allows a very sharp sweep angle to be adopted while providing plenty of depth for a simple but strong structure, and fuel tanks. Unlike traditional wings, it has no clearly defined point of stall but tends to bleed off speed at an alarming rate in a hard turn.*

Below: *The BAe Lightning featured a unique wing planform, with very sharp sweep on both leading and trailing edges and the ailerons on what can only be described as the wingtips, the main advantage being that they were at right angles to the airflow. The notch in the leading edge forms a vortex which does the same job as a wing fence.*

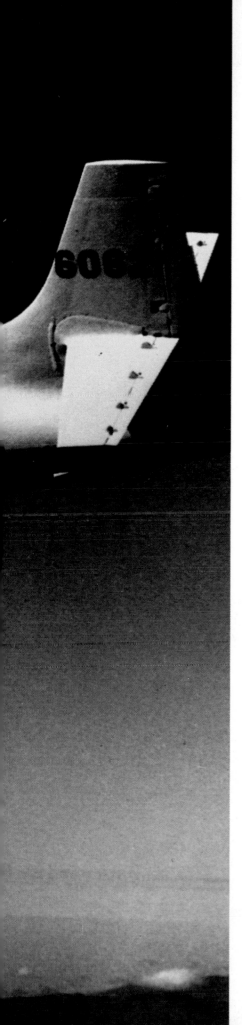

October 14

MACH 1

'Levelling off at 42,000 feet, I had thirty percent of my fuel, so I turned on rocket chamber three and immediately reached .96 Mach. I noticed that the faster I got, the smoother the ride. Suddenly the Mach needle began to fluctuate. It went up to .965 Mach — then tipped right off the scale... We were flying supersonic. And it was smooth as a baby's bottom; Grandma could be sitting up there sipping lemonade.'

GEN CHARLES 'CHUCK' YEAGER [27]

The Bell Experimental Sonic (XS)-1 was developed by the US National Advisory Committee for Aeronautics (NACA, later NASA) for research into transonic and supersonic flight. In 1944, when the program was launched, the newly emerging jet engine was opening up previously unexplored areas of high speed flight, and severe buffet and control problems were being encountered. Three XS-1s were ordered, to investigate these phenomena.

The XS-1 was modelled on the shape of the 0.50-caliber bullet, which was known to have excellent aerodynamic qualities, and given unswept but very thin wing and tail surfaces. It was powered by a four-chamber liquid-fuel rocket engine, which not only gave greater thrust than any jet of the period, but did not depend on external air for functioning.

Rocket motors use fuel at a prodigious rate, and to extend its endurance the XS-1 was air-launched at 25,000ft (7,620m) or more from a specially equipped Boeing B-29. The initial test flights were made by Bell test pilot Chalmers Goodlin, who explored the envelope up to Mach 0.80. At this point the Air Force took over, and the task fell to Mustang ace Chuck Yeager (inset).

Familiarization flights, with no fuel aboard, began in August 1947. The fourth flight, on August 29, was 'hot'. The assault on the so-called sound barrier had begun. Failure at this point could have ruined the entire program, so it was taken in easy stages, starting at Mach 0.82.

The XS-1 was unlike all other airplanes. The pilot sat semi-reclining, with his knees high. The view from the cockpit was poor, as the 'canopy' consisted simply of transparent panels which followed the shape of the fuselage. An emergency bale-out would probably result in the pilot hitting the sharp, knife-edged wing or tail surfaces. Behind the cockpit were fuel tanks containing alcohol and liquid oxygen, the chill from which reached through to the pilot. There was no heater and no defroster.

Gradually speeds were increased. Buffeting was encountered at Mach 0.86, and control was sluggish. Then, at Mach 0.94 on the seventh powered flight, the elevators ceased to function. This was overcome by using a trim switch to alter the angle of the stabilizers.

On the ninth powered flight Mach 0.97 was the target speed. As the laden B-29 clawed for altitude, Yeager climbed down the ladder from the bomber into the XS-1's cockpit, wherein was a length of broom handle. Yeager had broken two ribs two days before, and the broom was to be used as a lever to close the cockpit door.

Dropped at 20,000ft (6,100m), the XS-1 fell clear. Yeager fired the rockets and climbed like a bird. His own words, quoted above, tell the rest. The actual speed achieved was Mach 1.07. Man was supersonic!

BERLIN AIRLIFT

'Going into Tempelhof is a bit rough anyway. The pierced steel planking runway is bumpy… The approach from the west is like flying into a soup bowl. How I hate coming in over that damned Neukolln cemetery that looks like they put it there on purpose, with great apartment blocks flashing past the wingtips! If I overshoot, I finish up in the Russian sector.'

CAPT ANTHONY CECCHINI, USAF [28]

Following the end of the Second World War, the German capital, Berlin, which lay deep in the Soviet-occupied zone, was divided into four sectors, three of which were occupied by Western powers. This enclave of democracy in the heart of the Soviet zone was not relished by the Russians, who closed road and rail routes on June 24, 1948.

In retrospect it seems that the Soviet leadership calculated (rightly) that the Allies would not go to war for Berlin, but would tamely abandon a city which they could not keep supplied.

They were wrong. Three air corridors led to Berlin from the West, which the Russians could only close by armed intervention. The Allies therefore determined to supply Berlin entirely by air, in a massive and unprecedented display of air power. Called Operation Vittles by the Americans and Operation Plainfare by the British, the Berlin airlift was inaugurated on June 26, 1948.

At this stage, Berlin had supplies enough for six to eight weeks. The Soviets obviously calculated that the difficulties were insurmountable, and that all they had to do was wait. This seemed justified when, on the first day, a mere 80 tons (81.3 tonnes) of supplies were delivered.

Gradually more and more aircraft were brought into use, transferred from bases as diverse as Alaska and Hawaii, and including flying boats which landed on the Havelsee. Nor was it an entirely military operation. Aircraft from no fewer than 25 British companies took part. By July 20 supplies passed the 2,000 tons (2,030 tonnes) per day mark, and reached nearly 7,000 tons (7,100 tonnes) on September 18. Runways and taxiways were expanded by using rubble from bombsites (of which Berlin had plenty) and binding it with bitumen.

As ever more aircraft joined the airlift, air traffic problems became extreme. Spacings were often less than three minutes, with minimal altitude separation. With many different aircraft types, all with varying cruising speeds, extreme care had to be taken. Matters were not helped by Russian harrassment, of which 733 cases were recorded.

The airlift peaked on April 16, 1949, when no less than 12,940 tons (13,140 tonnes) were flown into the beleagured city. Shortly after, on May 12, the Soviet blockade was lifted, although the airlift continued until September 30. The statistics were staggering: 692 aircraft flew 277,804 flights, delivering 2.32 million tons (2.35 million tonnes) of supplies — not only food, but coal and fuel oil as well. This was not achieved without cost. Seventeen fatal accidents occurred, with the loss of 18 British and 31 American lives, and there were many close shaves.

The Berlin airlift revealed a hitherto unsuspected dimension of air power; that an aggressor could be faced down without resort to armed force.

July 16

TURBOPROP

'... Your seat pushes you firmly in the back. Even then there is none of the shuddering brazen bellow of the high-powered piston engine... Combined with a seemingly uncanny lack of vibration, this gives the impression almost of sailing through space, the engines with their glinting propeller discs utterly remote from the quiet security of this cabin.'

DEREK HARVEY[29]

The above passage was the impression of a passenger taking his first ride in a Vickers-Armstrongs Viscount airliner powered by four Rolls-Royce Dart turboprops.

While air travel has always been fast and convenient, in the early years it was uncomfortable and fatiguing to a degree that would be unbelievable to modern travellers accustomed to jets. The only form of power available was the piston engine, which, in spite of the best attempts at soundproofing, was noisy enough to make conversation difficult, and which also set up a continuous vibration throughout the airframe which could be distinctly felt by the passengers.

Reciprocating engines vibrated because they had a lot of parts going up and down. During the Second World War the jet engine was developed. Instead of pistons and con-rods going up and down, motive power was provided by a turbine which went round and round, with a noticeable absence of vibration.

The jet engine is at its most efficient at high altitudes and speeds, making it ideal for long-range flight. For medium-range work it was less than optimum. A compromise solution was to couple a propeller to the turbine shaft through a gearbox, to produce a turboprop engine.

The Viscount was designed for medium range and economic cruising speed, and the choice of a turboprop seems now to have been obvious. It was, however, the first civilian airliner to be so powered.

The first flight took place at Wisley on July 16, 1948, with veteran test pilot 'Mutt' Summers at the controls. Not only was the flight uneventful, but the subsequent flying program was almost entirely troublefree. The Viscount's first appearance at the Farnborough Air Show the next year was notable for its quietness. Certificated on July 28, 1950, it flew its first scheduled passenger service the following day.

The original V.630 Viscount design seated no more than 40 passengers, but greater capacity was needed. To provide this, the fuselage was stretched to form the V.700 series, seating up to 53. This variant was immediately ordered by British European Airways, and other orders started to trickle in.

So popular was the type in service, not only for its quietness and comfort but for its large oval windows, that the trickle swelled to a flood. Remarkably, it was even bought by American airlines, who could find nothing homegrown.

The Viscount was also used to set class records; London-Cologne, etc. The V.700 prototype also took part in the London to New Zealand Air Race of 1953, becoming the first transport aircraft to finish.

The final Viscount series was the V.800, a slightly stretched aircraft seating up to 70. The Viscount, of which 444 were built, was the first of a new generation.

1949
July 27

JET AIRLINER

'Millions wonder what it is like to travel in the Comet at 500 miles an hour eight miles above the earth. Paradoxically there is a sensation of being poised motionless in space. Because of the great height the scene below scarcely appears to move; because of the stability of the atmosphere the aircraft remains rock-steady... One arrives over distant landmarks in an incredibly short time but without the sense of having travelled. Speed does not enter into the picture. One doubts one's wristwatch.'

C. MARTIN SHARP [30]

The above description will be entirely familiar to anyone used to modern jet travel, but when these words were written, in 1949, they were new and fresh, a paean of joy celebrating the opening of a whole new era. The era of jet travel.

The first jet airliner, de Havilland's Comet 1, was rolled out in April 1949. Resplendent in shiny aluminum, it was a sleek cigar shape into which the windows of the crew cabin were smoothly faired. Four de Havilland Ghost turbojets were buried in the wing roots, adding to the impression of speed and grace.

The first flight took place on July 27. At the controls was former night fighter ace John Cunningham, now de Havilland's chief test pilot. His first reaction was one of surprise at the acceleration, which was exceptional for such a large machine. Handling qualities were good, and a year of intensive flight testing followed, during which many international point-to-point speed records were set.

So impressive were these that orders started to come in, not only from the British Overseas Airways Corporation, but also from Canada and France. Then, on May 2, 1952, the first scheduled Comet service left Heathrow with a full complement of 36 passengers. After stops at Rome, Beirut, Khartoum, Entebbe, and Livingstone, Comet G-ALYP 'Yoke Peter' arrived at Johannesburg two minutes ahead of schedule after 23 1/2 hours and 6,774 statute miles (10,900km).

The initial success of the Comet 1 sparked more interest, and orders now came from Japan and South America. By this time the Comet 2, powered by Rolls-Royce engines and with 44 seats and longer range, was under development, and a stretched version, the Comet 3, with 78 seats, was projected. With no immediate competitors in sight, the Comet looked like being a runaway success.

But all was not roses. The record was marred by two take-off

accidents, one at Ciampino, Rome, and another at Karachi, in Pakistan. While the verdict on both was pilot error, a new high-lift wing section was proposed. Then, exactly a year after the inauguration of the London to Johannesburg service, disaster struck.

Comet 'Yoke Victor', en route from Calcutta to Delhi, broke up in mid-air. Close investigation revealed no weaknesses, and the cause remained a mystery. Then, on January 15, 1954, 'Yoke Peter' broke up near Elba. Again the cause was a mystery, but when on April 8 'Yoke Yoke' fell into the Bay of Naples, the fleet was grounded.

The truth was that the Comet had been too far ahead of its time, and had fallen victim to the then little-known phenomenon of metal fatigue. It had pioneered the way, and had paid a high price, although the knowledge gained was to benefit every airliner that followed it. The final variant, the Comet 4, gave years of troublefree service.

April 15

THE BIG STICK

'... I felt a drop in the seat of my pants, as though the nose had fallen. It was the pilot pushing down to avoid the missile. I turned and looked at the instruments. The altimeter was shooting through 700ft (213m), and we were doing about 440kt (815km/hr), heading down fast. At 500ft (152m) I grabbed the yoke and started pulling. The plane being heavy with fuel, it was just not responding. I was sure we were going to hit. The plane eventually dished out at 60ft (18m) above the ground.'

CAPT CARL GRAMLICK, USAF [31]

The Boeing B-52 Stratofortress is, as a design, older than its oldest crewman, and probably older than many of its crewmen's fathers. It was conceived in the early days of the Cold War, when strategic bombing was fashionable and an all-out war between the Soviet Union and the West seemed not only possible, but probable. For many years it was one leg of the nuclear triad, the others being intercontinental ballistic missiles and missile submarines. It was in fact part of the ultimate deterrent; the 'Big Stick.'

The B-52 was initially planned as a straight-winged bomber powered by six turboprop engines. While a jet bomber would have been more survivable on account of its greater speed, the early jet engines were too prodigal of fuel to meet the stringent range requirement of 10,000 miles (16,000km).

The change to jets came about because of the increasing importance placed on flight refueling at that time. The design was revised, and emerged with eight turbojets slung below a shoulder-set wing swept to an angle of 35°. The detonation in 1949 of the first Soviet nuclear weapon hurried the program along, and the preproduction YB-52 first flew on April 15, 1952.

Externally it resembled the smaller B-47 Stratojet, which at one point was the most numerous aircraft in US Strategic Air Command (SAC), but in fact it was considerably different. Few changes were made during the development period, although the tandem cockpit initially adopted gave way to a roomy airliner-style 'office.'

The first production B-52 left the ground on August 5, 1954, and the type started reaching the Bombardment Wings in June 1955. Production continued for ten years, a total of 744 machines of all marks being built. For the next three decades the SAC B-52s provided a nuclear shield for the free world. The six-man crew included a gunner, in a tail turret. In later variants he was given a remote position in the fuselage.

The B-52 had been designed to operate high in the stratosphere, but the increasing effectiveness of Soviet air defenses forced a change to low level. A structural rework was needed to cope with the harsh low-level environment. This was underlined in 1964, when a B-52H lost most of its vertical stabilizer in flight owing to a wind gust of incredible severity, although it returned safely to base.

For many years the B-52 flew in the manned penetrator role, using Quail decoys and Hound Dog missiles (main picture), before it was supplanted by the B-1B Lancer. It then became a stand-off-missile launcher. In the more conventional bombing role it gave sterling service in Vietnam (inset), and again in the Gulf War of 1991, where it flew raids direct from Diego Garcia, England, and finally from the continental United States.

Left: *An unusual, but recognizable, view of a B-52 Stratofortress coming in to land with wheels and flaps extended. As can be seen, the main gear trucks are housed in the fuselage fore and aft of the capacious weapons bay, while outriggers are mounted towards the wingtips. ASQ-151 Electro-optical Viewing System blisters beneath the nose mark this aircraft as a B-52H.*

Above: *The nearest Russian equivalent to the B-52 was the Tupolev Tu-95/142, reporting name Bear. First flown in 1954, it had the unusual combination of swept wings and turboprop engines, and was used for long-range missions. Seen here is a TU-95 Bear D maritime reconnaissance variant, being escorted off the premises, politely but firmly, by two Iceland-based USAF F-15s.*

Below: *The Avro Vulcan was the British 'big stick' for many years. First flown on August 30, 1952, it was a tailless delta designed for high-speed, high-altitude penetration. Unlike the B-52 and Tu-95, it did not carry a tail gun, depending on a combination of high performance and electronic counter-measures (ECM) for survival. It remained in service with the RAF until 1992.*

1953
October 24

ROBOT FIGHTER

'... one of the best gadgets was the Tactical Situation Display Indicator that sat between your knees like a little round television set. You could put in any number of film strip combinations of maps and navigate all over the world with a complete picture of the terrain, landmarks, airfields, and navigation aids constantly unfolding and updating in front of you. For air-to-air combat situations there was even a nice-looking little moving bug that was you and an ugly little moving bug that was your adversary.'

COL JACK BROUGHTON, USAF (RET) [32]

The Cold War saw the emergence of a new threat to the United States; very fast, high-flying bombers attacking over the North Pole, armed with nuclear weapons. These had to be intercepted as far away as possible by day and by night, given that daylight is minimal during the winter months in northerly latitudes.

The traditional pursuit course interception was difficult and time consuming, and the USAF set out to find something better. The solution was collision course interception. In this the fighter headed directly toward the bomber, and launched its weapons as soon as it came within range.

In anything other than clear air and daylight, the fighter had to attack without making visual contact. Airborne radar, previously used solely for detection, was now expanded into an automatic fire control system (FCS), coupled to the autopilot. Vectored out under close ground control, the fighter would

acquire a target on radar; the system would lead it in the right direction, and the weapons would be launched at the optimum moment.

The first fighter designed from the outset for automatic interception was the Convair F-102A Delta Dagger (inset, top left), which first flew on October 24, 1953. A large but trim tailless delta, it could, after initial teething troubles had been cured, reach Mach 1.25, and carried six AIM-4 Falcon missiles in an internal bay.

The FCS was to have been the Hughes MX-1179, but development was delayed and the less capable MG-3 replaced it. The F-102A entered service in the spring of 1956, and 873 reached USAF squadrons.

The next step was the F-102B, an extensively redesigned F-102A with a more powerful engine which enabled it to reach Mach 2.31, while the FCS was the far more capable Hughes MA-1. This could be tied into the Semi-Automatic Ground

Environment (SAGE) system which covered the northern approaches to the continental USA. Data link could be used for steering instructions to bring the fighter to a point where its onboard systems could make contact with the target.

The F-102B was redesignated F-106 and named Delta Dart (left and inset, right: firing Genie). The pilot was responsible for take off and landing, arming the weapons, monitoring the fuel state, and not much else. It was the nearest thing to a robot fighter yet built.

Despite the high level of automation, the F-106 was popular with its pilots. To return to Jack Broughton:

'Just for fun, you could set up on final for landing and keep pulling that nose up until she was in a full stall. Then you could ride that stall through a 1,000ft (305m) drop, still with full lateral control, then lower the nose a tad and touch down within a few feet of where you wanted to.' [33]

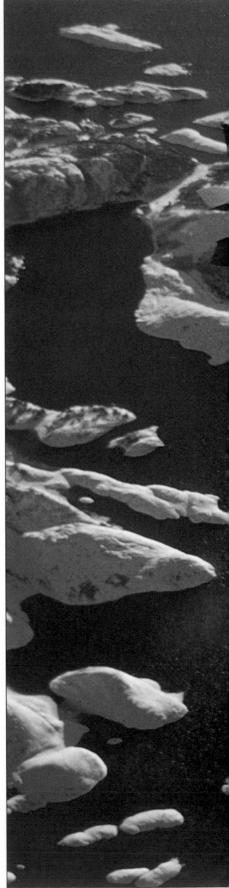

Above: *The automatic interceptor as typified by the F-106 was very much a single-mission aircraft. It was eclipsed in USAF service by the F-4 Phantom, a true multi-mission machine which proved its worth in many conflicts around the world. Seen here is an F-4E of the 347th Tactical Fighter Wing (TFW).*

Left: *The Soviet Union also embraced the automated fighter concept with the Mikoyan MiG-25, reporting name Foxbat. As with the F-106, the pilot was a system manager, with the interception controled from the ground via data link. With a maximum speed of Mach 2.8, Foxbat was the fastest fighter in the world.*

Right: *Three F-15C Eagles of the 36th Fighter Wing from Bitburg, Germany, patrol over an Arctic seascape. The F-15, with its complement of beyond-visual-range and close-combat missiles, has an enviable record in air combat, gained in both USAF and considerable Israeli service.*

FASTEST AND HIGHEST

'As I blasted towards the heavens, I alternated between side-arm control and centre stick, pumping in tentative control motions to feel her out. Even then the X-15 remained firm and stable. I stared in fascination at the Machmeter, which climbed quickly from Mach 1.5 to Mach 1.8, and then effortlessly to my top speed for this flight, Mach 2.3...'

SCOTT CROSSFIELD [34]

Since the first powered flight, the quest had been for ever greater speeds and altitudes. It reached its apogee with the North American X-15 hypersonic research aircraft. Like the earlier Bell XS-1, the X-15 was air-launched from a modified Boeing B-52.

Intended to explore a speed/altitude range of Mach 5+/50 miles (80km), the X-15 was powered by a rocket motor giving 57,000lb (25,855kg) of static thrust on a mix of liquid oxygen and anhydrous ammonia. Special chrome-nickel alloys were used to offset extremes of aerodynamic heating; and three control systems were provided: a conventional center-stick for landing; a side stick (anticipating the General Dynamics F-16 by more than a decade) for launch, acceleration, and climb-out; and a reaction system using hydrogen peroxide thrusters for control at very high altitude.

The first flight, on June 8, 1959, was unpowered. Dropped from 40,000ft (12,191m), the X-15 handled well until the final approach, when the nose suddenly pitched up. Test pilot Scott Crossfield tried to catch it, but got out of phase with the system, which was too sensitive. The result was a porpoising motion. However, he succeeded in making a good if fairly heavy landing at the bottom of an oscillation.

The first 'hot' flight took place on September 17, albeit with an engine less powerful than that intended. Crossfield commented, 'It was immediately apparent that we had built a beautiful airplane. Its nose held straight and firm without the yaw and pitch common to most high-performance airplanes.'

Inevitably problems arose, but these were gradually overcome, and the definitive XLR99 motor was fitted to the #2 aircraft. On the first flight with the new powerplant, on November 15, 1960, Crossfield reached Mach 2.97 at 81,200ft (24,749m). Shortly after this the North American flight program was concluded, and the X-15s were turned over to the National Aeronautics and Space Administration (NASA), the USAF and USN.

Over the next few years a dazzling series of flights took place, as the X-15s explored the flight envelope. NASA test pilot Joe Walker reached 246,700ft (75,190m) on April 30, 1962, then on August 22, 1963, took the third X-15 up to 354,200ft (107,955m), slightly more than 67 miles; an altitude never since exceeded by a winged aircraft. Space begins 50 miles (80km) above the Earth's surface.

Nor was speed neglected. Air Force pilot Bob White reached Mach 4.43 on March 7, 1961, exceeded Mach 5 on June 23, and then, on November 9, flying at 101,600ft (30,966m), attained Mach 6.04.

Meanwhile, the # 2 aircraft had been rebuilt as the X-15A-2, and in this machine Maj William Knight reached Mach 6.72 on October 3, 1967 (inset). After 199 flights, the program ended on October 24, 1968.

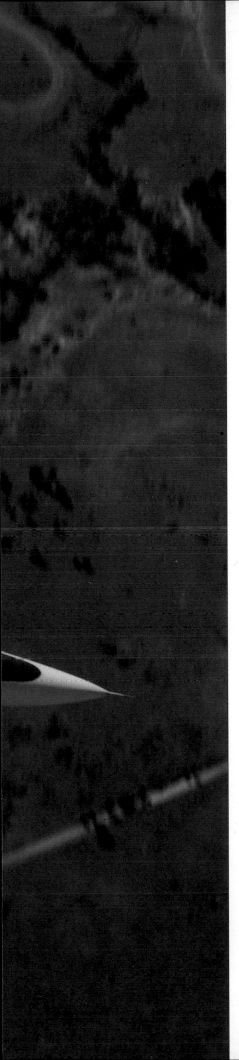

December 21

SWING WINGS

'I'm not sure if anyone really knows what the F-111's top speed is. On my first flight in the F-111 we reached Mach 2 while climbing out from takeoff, still relatively heavy, and had to reduce speed only to keep from running out of the supersonic corridor. A nice turn was made at 1.8, and the aircraft performed exceedingly well (turns, rolls etc) while supersonic. It is designed to provide a stable bombing platform while supersonic on the deck, and it does this very well.'

MAJ PETER DUNN, USAF[35]

Aircraft design consists of a series of compromises. A short-span, highly-swept wing is optimum for high speed flight, especially in the bumpy air encountered at low level, whereas a long-span, straight wing allows economical cruising, higher ceiling, and most importantly, slower take-off and landing speeds, reducing the runway length required.

What was obviously needed was a method of varying the wing sweep in flight. Like all aviation ideas, this dated back many years. The first variable-sweep aircraft to fly was the Westland Pterodactyl IV, in March 1931. It was a modest beginning, as the variation in sweep was a mere 4.75°, and was intended only to trim the aircraft for different loads.

Next in the field were the Germans, but the Second World War ended before any flight trials could be made. The aircraft in question, the Messerschmitt P.1101, was shipped to the USA after the war, where it became the basis for the

first true variable-sweep aircraft, the Bell X-5. It was in this aircraft, on June 27, 1951, that Bell test pilot Skip Ziegler first changed the sweep of the wings from 20° to 50° in flight.

Next came the Grumman XF10F-1 Jaguar (inset), in which Corky Meyer experienced some moments most kindly described as 'interesting'. The main problem was that the wing had to move through its full range of sweep without significantly moving the aerodynamic center. This could be done, but the mechanism was heavy and mechanically complex.

The idea lapsed, to be revived when NASA discovered that having a separate pivot point for each wing, mounted outboard and slightly aft of the normal location, would produce acceptable characteristics. Coincident with this came the USAF Specific Operational Requirement (SOR) 183 for a multi-role tactical fighter, the performance and handling demands of which could best be met by variable sweep.

The contract was eventually won by General Dynamics with what became the F-111, which first flew on December 21, 1964. With this, swing-wing aircraft could truly be said to have come of age.

This was far from the end of the story. The F-111 was unable to fulfil the fighter role, and was plagued by technical problems. But at minimum sweep it could get off the ground in a reasonable distance with a heavy load of ordnance, cruise economically for long distances, and then, with wings swept back, give a stable ride at supersonic speeds in the dense air close to the ground. The addition of terrain-following radar coupled to the autopilot allowed this to be done in total darkness or bad weather.

After an inauspicious combat debut in Vietnam, the F-111 clearly demonstrated its unsurpassed capabilities later in that war. Although the design was elderly by the time of the Gulf War in 1991, the type remained extremely effective.

Above: *France entered the swing-wing field in 1967 with the Mirage G, and followed it four years later with the Mirage G.8. The latter was built in both single- and two-seat versions; both are shown above. Further progress was abandoned in favor of a different design, the swept-wing Mirage F.1.*

Below: *The Soviet Union produced many swing-wing types, the most prolific of all being the Mikoyan MiG-23, which was built in both interceptor and attack versions. Three wing settings were used; minimum for take-off and landing, intermediate for maneuver combat, and full sweep for maximum speed.*

Right: *Grumman's F-14A Tomcat is the most potent swing-wing fighter ever built. Computerized wing sweep automatically gives the optimum setting for every combination of speed/altitude, and it is fully maneuverable at all settings. AIM-54 AAMs give it an unmatched kill capability.*

Left: *The only European swing-wing aircraft to enter service is the Tornado , built by a tri-national consortium composed of Britain, Germany and Italy. Conceived as an interdictor/strike aircraft, the Tornado was given swing wings to provide good short-field performance and low gust response for a smooth ride at low level. It was later modified for the interceptor mission for the RAF as the Tornado F.3, two examples of which are shown here. Minimum sweep not only gives good short-field performance, but allows an extended loiter time on patrol while far out over the North Sea. As with the Tomcat, wing sweep is automatically scheduled to give the optimum angle in all flight conditions. At low speeds, with all high-lift devices deployed, it is remarkably agile.*

Above: *Swing wings are not only the province of the fighter and attack aircraft; they can also be used for much larger aircraft. Shown here is the Rockwell B-1B Lancer, a strategic bomber of which over 90 are in service with the USAF. The mission profile of the Lancer is to operate from short austere airstrips, cruise out at economic speeds and medium altitudes, then refuel in flight before penetrating hostile air-space at ultra-low level and high subsonic speeds, under the enemy radar coverage. The ability to alter wing sweep is crucial to flying this very demanding mission. There is just one swing-wing aircraft larger than Lancer. This is the Tupolev Tu-160, NATO reporting name Blackjack. Very few of these have entered Russian service, and production has ceased.*

December 22

ULTIMATE SPYPLANE

'...we were in a continuous shroud of high thick cirrus which extended to the mid-sixties [thousands of feet]. We were moving at Mach 2.6 when we blasted from the cloud tops. It was like being shot from a rocket as we bolted from the high tropopause into the clear stratosphere. We did another fast circuit of North Vietnam... then descended back into Thailand where the other storms had been.'

MAJ DON WALBRECHT, USAF [36]

It was as a reconnaissance vehicle that the aircraft first proved its worth in war. Survival lay in great speed, great altitude, or a combination of both. The SR-71 Blackbird, a product of Lockheed's famed 'Skunk Works', was the greatest of this breed. In a Service career spanning a quarter of a century it proved totally uninterceptable.

The predecessor of the SR-71, the Lockheed U-2, flew at moderate speeds and used very high altitudes to evade interception. That this was not enough was demonstrated on May 1, 1960, when a U-2 was brought down inside the Soviet Union by a surface-to-air missile (SAM).

Greater altitudes were an obvious need, but overwhelming speed was the real solution. Not only would this make interception by a manned fighter tremendously difficult, but it would crimp in the engagement envelope of even the most capable SAM. The difference between the 450kt (834km/hr) of the U-2 and the Mach 3 of the SR-71 reduced the time available for missile engagement by 75% and demanded four times greater accuracy from the weapon's guidance system.

First flown on December 22, 1964, the SR-71 was developed from the A-12. Optimized for sustained cruise at Mach 3 at 80,000ft (24,383m), it was built mainly of titanium to withstand the kinetic heating of prolonged supersonic flight. A tailless delta wing carried two huge J58 turbo-ramjets located outboard. This layout had the advantage of keeping boundary layer air away from the sensitive intakes, but at the cost of poor asymmetric handling qualities in the event of power loss on one side. Other features were inward-canted twin fins and a pronounced chine along each side of the nose, both contributing to a reduced radar cross-section.

The SR-71 entered service in January 1966. In all, 32 were delivered, including two SR-71B trainers, distinguishable by their raised rear cockpits.

For many years Blackbirds flew reconnaissance missions, operating mainly out of Beale AFB in California, Mildenhall in Suffolk, England, and Kadena on Okinawa. North Vietnam was frequently visited, and overflights of Egypt and other Middle Eastern countries were made during and after the October War of 1973. The aircraft used a special high-density fuel, JP-7, and thus needed dedicated tanker support for longer missions, which could last up to ten hours.

The SR-71 is credited with the ability to scan more than 100,000sq miles (259,000sq km) of the Earth's surface every hour. It could therefore probe the Soviet air defenses from international airspace. Lt Viktor Belenko, a MiG-25 pilot based at Chuguyevka in the Far East, reported many unsuccessful attempts to intercept SR-71s. The final flight of the incomparable SR-71 took place on March 6, 1990.

1965
September 7

ATTACK HELO

'I tried to slow down the attacking force in the field with rockets and 20mm cannon fire. I had never seen several hundred men in the open before, so I was in hog heaven... I slowed to about 40kt (74km/hr) and opened up with the twenty. I was having a great time, the 20mm was tearing them to shreds, and I continued my run all the way to about 30ft (9m) and then broke to the left over the river.'

CAPT TERRYL MORRIS [37]

In its early days the army helicopter was regarded very much as a utility machine that could be adapted for various missions by a simple change of equipment. While the flexibility bestowed by this arrangement was in many ways a tremendous advantage, the use of rotary-winged aircraft in the battle zone inevitably suggested that an offensive capability was possible.

A few helicopters were fitted with *ad hoc* weapons in Korea, and by the French in Indo-China, but it was not until the French-Algerian War of 1954-1962 that helicopters equipped for the fire-support mission emerged.

The next war of note was the 'in-country war' in Vietnam, where helicopters were used on a vast scale in air cavalry operations. While transport machines routinely carried door gunners, these were insufficient to suppress ground fire, and other helicopters of the same type were armed and flown as gunships. This, however, was only a temporary solution; what was really needed was a helicopter dedicated to the task.

This duly emerged as the Bell AH-1 HueyCobra, the first flight of which took place on September 7, 1965, when tested as the Model 209 (main picture). The proven dynamics of the UH-1 were married to a new narrow body which reduced presented area and drag, and gave its two-man crew a much better all-round view. They sat in tandem, with the pilot behind the gunner. Stub wings were introduced to provide attachment points for a heavy load of weapons, and they also unloaded the rotor in fast forward flight, increasing agility. A degree of armor protection was provided to reduce vulnerability.

Armament initially comprised a 7.62mm Minigun in a traversing chin turret, pods of unguided rockets and grenade launchers, although the gun was quickly replaced by a far more effective 20mm cannon.

The HueyCobra reached Vietnam in mid-1968, and quickly proved its worth (inset, left). Later variants had flat-plate canopy transparencies to reduce sun glint, more power, and a much wider variety of weaponry which included anti-tank missiles, enabling it to be used in the anti-armor role. As the SuperCobra and SeaCobra it is used by the USMC, Israel and Iran, while armed with Sidewinder or Stinger air-to-air missiles it can be used in the anti-helicopter role.

The HueyCobra is important because it pioneered the attack helicopter concept and proved it in action. The layout has become standardized; a two-man crew with the gunner in front of the pilot, angular flat transparencies, stub wings to carry ordnance loads, and armor for protection.

There are other, newer attack helicopters in service, of which the AH-64 Apache is probably the best known, but variants of the Cobra are still around in large numbers (inset, right), and most recently gave sterling service in the Gulf War.

Left: *A Russian Mil Mi-24 Hind D lets fly with an AT-2 Swatter anti-tank guided missile. Hind D is an assault helicopter, fast, heavily armed and armored, and with room for eight fully-armed troops in the cabin. Missile reloads are an alternative cargo. Hind D saw extensive service in Afghanistan, where it gained a formidable reputation.*

Below: *Kamov's Ka-50 Werewolf is unique among attack helicopters in that it is a single-seater, and has an ejection seat for the pilot. The twin contra-rotating rotors make it particularly easy to handle, as this eliminates the torque effect common to single-rotor types. Displayed at Le Bourget in 1993, it appeared very agile, but the workload for the pilot must be very high.*

Right: *Arguably the most deadly battlefield helicopter in service is the McDonnell Douglas AH-64 Apache, which played a vital role in the Gulf War of 1991. First flown on September 30, 1975, it carries an unparalleled range of sensors for target location, tracking and attack, and is fully night-capable. The latest model is the AH-64D, which carries Longbow milimeter-wave radar on a mast-mounted sight.*

Below: *The attack helicopter of the future is the RAH-66 Comanche developed by Boeing-Sikorsky, and seen here in mockup form. Stealth technology has been extensively used to lower acoustic, radar, visual, and infrared signatures to make it less detectable. All anti-tank and air-to-air missiles are carried internally.*

JUMP JET

'I recall very vividly my first press-up. The airplane became a cork out of a champagne bottle; it was headed straight up very rapidly and I had a lot of trouble getting the power off, so that I didn't end up on instruments in the hover. I found the hovering aspects of it intoxicating, and they finally had to tell me to come down, I enjoyed it so much.'

COL TOM MILLER, USMC[38]

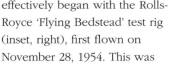

The first production Hawker Siddeley (later British Aerospace) Harrier flew on December 28, 1967, and the type entered squadron service with the RAF in the following year, to become the world's first vertical take-off and landing (VTOL) warplane.

Immediate interest was shown by the US Marine Corps, who sent a three-man team to Farnborough in September 1968, one of whom was Col Tom Miller, whose account is given above. The USMC has since become the major user of the Harrier, under the designation AV-8.

The ability to take off and land vertically, while retaining the attributes of a conventional airplane, had long been a dream. Only with the advent of the jet engine did the combination of power and light weight become available.

Exploration of the VTOL regime effectively began with the Rolls-Royce 'Flying Bedstead' test rig (inset, right), first flown on November 28, 1954. This was

followed by other test rigs in Germany and Russia.

The first VTOL aircraft were tail-sitters such as the Ryan X-13 Vertijet. Take off was not too bad, but landing vertically backwards posed enormous problems. The 'flat riser' looked more promising, and this was the next step.

The obvious way of producing a flat riser was to install a number of lift jets, plus a separate engine for forward flight. This was not terribly efficient, as the lift jets were dead weight throughout most of the mission. An alternative solution, pioneered by Hawker Aircraft and Bristol Siddeley engines, was vectored thrust, whereby one large engine exhausted through four swivelling nozzles.

The initial result was the Hawker P.1127 (inset, left), which started tethered hovering trials on October 21, 1960. This was followed by the Kestrel, a more workmanlike machine of limited operational usefulness, which was eventually

developed to become the Harrier.

In the close air support role the Harrier can be based forward, giving it a very rapid reaction time, although keeping it supplied is a major logistics problem. For this reason it has not been sold abroad as much as was once hoped.

Its short take-off/vertical landing (STOVL) qualities, however, allow it to be operated from quite small ships, and in its Sea Harrier guise its air combat qualities were convincingly demonstrated in the Falklands conflict of 1982.

While the Harrier is not supersonic, and not particularly agile in conventional flight, vectoring the nozzles in flight allows some very unorthodox maneuvers to be performed which make it a formidable opponent in close combat. The most recent fighter variant is the Harrier II Plus (at left is the GR.7), which is equipped with the Hughes APG-65 radar and carries AIM-120 Amraam missiles, as does the British Sea Harrier FRS.2.

Left, top: *The Bell XV-5A was a moderately successful attempt at producing a VTOL aircraft, in that it at least flew. Developed for the US Army, it used a 'fan-in-wing' system for vertical lift. In this sequence, taken at Edwards AFB on November 17, 1964, it can be seen rising vertically, then slowly transitioning to forward flight. Butterfly doors cover the fans in conventional flight; these can be seen in the open position.*

Left, bottom: *The Sea Harrier FRS.2 is the latest variant for the Royal Navy. It is seen here armed with four AIM-120 Amraam AAMs, and carries the compatible Blue Vixen pulse-Doppler radar in an extended nose. In the South Atlantic conflict of 1982, the STOVL capability of the Sea Harrier enabled it to operate in weather too bad for conventional carrier aircraft.*

Right, top: *The vectored-thrust capability of the Harrier can be used for things other than take-off and landing. When used at combat speeds in conventional wingborne flight, it can produce some very unorthodox maneuvers. No conventional machine can stay behind a Harrier once it decides to decelerate, which is what is happening in this strange time-exposed picture, in which the nozzles can be seen at almost 90° deflection.*

Right: *The AV-8B Harrier II Night Attack prototype is seen here fitted with pods, that on the port side housing a five-barrel 25mm cannon, and the starboard pod holding 300 rounds of ammunition. The missiles are AGM-65 Mavericks.*

February 9

WIDEBODY

'Pilot Jack Waddell eased throttles forward; Co-Pilot Brien Wygle called out speeds as a gentle giant of the air began to move; Flight Engineer Jess Wallick kept eyes glued to gauges. The Boeing Model 747 Superjet gathered speed. The nose lifted. After 4,300ft — less than half the 9,000ft runway — main gear of the plane left the concrete. At 11.34 a.m., with a speed of 164 miles an hour, quietly and almost serenely, the age of spacious jets began.'

BOEING MAGAZINE [39]

The Boeing 747, familiarly known as the 'Jumbo Jet,' set a new trend in air travel as the first of the widebody airliners. This came about less by intent than by a series of happy coincidences.

In the mid-1960s Boeing was a hive of activity, turning out airliners and commercial transports by the score. Four-jet 707s and 717s, and tri-jet 727s, were all in production, and the short-range twin-jet 737 was coming along nicely. The company had lost the USAF C-5 military transport contract to Lockheed, but was working on an SST (supersonic transport) which it confidently expected would sweep the board in the future.

At the time container ships were proving a huge success. Boeing felt that there was a niche in the market for a long-range freighter which would add the advantage of speed to the covenience of container handling. Drawing on their experience with the abortive C-5 project, the company produced a design wide enough to permit two 8ft (2.44m) wide containers side by side, and it was this, rather than any other factor, which resulted in the first widebody jet.

Further research showed that the projected growth in passenger traffic would require greater capacity. One advantage of a really large airplane was that costs per seat-mile or per ton-mile would be considerably reduced, whereas those of the SST (already the object of doubts about its viability) would be much higher. Consequently, the Boeing 747 was designed to serve as a passenger transport with ten-abreast seating, as a freighter, or as a combination of the two. On April 13, 1966, long before the first flight, Pan American Airways signed a contract for two cargo aircraft and 23 airliners configured to carry 350 to 400 passengers.

On February 9, 1969, the flight test crew of pilot Jack Waddell, copilot Brien Wygle and flight engineer Jess Wallick lifted the huge machine into the air for the first time at Paine Field. The 747 was remarkably quiet by the standards of the day, while its enormous size belied its speed, making it seem to hang in the air. That first flight was uneventful, as was the succeeding test program, and the aircraft was awarded FAA certification at the end of that same year.

Shortly after, on January 22, 1970, Pam Am made the inaugural flight with the type from New York to Heathrow. Since then, more than 1,000 Boeing 747s have been completed in many variants. Engines are provided by Rolls-Royce, Pratt & Whitney or General Electric according to operator's choice; passenger accommodation varies between 366 and 550, while maximum take-off weight is 833,000lb (377,850kg).

Cruising at speeds in excess of 500kt (925km/hr) at altitudes of up to 45,000ft (13,715m), this superb machine will be with us for many years to come.

CONCORDE

'The sun is now climbing from the west. In winter it is possible to leave London after sunset, on the evening Concorde for New York, and watch the sun rise out of the west. Flying at Mach 2 at these latitudes will cause the sun to set in the west at three times its normal rate, casting, as it does so, a vast curved shadow of the earth, up and ahead of the aircraft.'

FIRST OFFICER CHRISTOPHER ORLEBAR[40]

The above is fairly typical of the commentary given to passengers on the London/New York Concorde service. Other comments are that the cruising speed of Mach 2 covers a mile every 2.75 seconds, and that the cruising altitude is twice the height of Mount Everest, where the sky looks much darker, almost black, and on a clear day the curvature of the Earth can just be made out.

Concorde, the result of Anglo-French collaboration, is the world's only supersonic airliner, operated only by British Airways and Air France. In service with the former it can typically carry 100 passengers from London Heathrow to New York J.F. Kennedy in less than three-and-a-half hours. This is rather faster than the change in time zones, with the amusing result that arrival time in New York is more than an hour earlier than the departure time in London.

In the 1950s aircraft performance increased faster than ever before.

While this was mainly applicable to military aviation, the possibility of building a supersonic transport (SST) looked increasingly attractive.

The Anglo-French agreement which led to Concorde was signed in November 1962. Within a year the USA announced that it, too, would develop an SST, while the Soviet Union also determined not to be left behind.

The American SST was intended to be larger and faster than its European rival and, therefore, would have been far more expensive. It eventually foundered on the twin rocks of technology and finance. The Russian Tupolev Tu-144 (inset), dubbed 'Concordski' owing to its superficial resemblance to the Anglo-French aircraft, was of similar size to it, with a 'paper performance' slightly better.

The Tu-144 was the first SST to fly, some two months ahead of Concorde, on December 3, 1968. On June 5, 1969, it went supersonic for the first time, and on May 26, 1970,

it exceeded Mach 2. In both cases it was a few months ahead of Concorde.

A radically revised Tu-144 appeared at Le Bourget in 1973, but crashed during its display. The type was used by Aeroflot from December 1975 on the Moscow-Kazakshtan run, but was withdrawn from service on June 1, 1978.

By contrast, Concorde first flew on March 2, 1969, piloted by Andre Turcat, began passenger services on January 21, 1976, and has been flying continually every since. It would have been one of the greatest success stories in aviation history had it not been for one unforeseen factor.

The impact of vociferous environmental groups made it increasingly difficult to obtain routes to the USA, and these were the ones that counted. These were finally granted, but too late to help sales. The result was that only 20 Concordes were built, of which 16 were production models.

—1974—
January 20

SUPER-AGILITY

'The angle is about ninety degrees and the MiG's silvery body is every fighter pilot's dream. The missile slides off the left wing… Five seconds pass — they seem an eternity — until the missile explodes with a small plume of smoke. Contact. The MiG simply stands still in the air. Another second and his right wing is suddenly torn from place; the aircraft spins and catches fire.'

MAJ R, ISRAELI F-16 PILOT [41]

In the late 1960s the major perceived threat to the free world was all-out war in Central Europe against the Soviet Union and her allies, against vastly superior numbers in the air. The seriousness of this was underlined in Vietnam, where the latest US fighters had been forced into close combat, a role for which they had never been designed, by light and agile Russian-built aircraft.

The latest US air superiority fighters were unaffordable in the numbers necessary. A Pentagon group later known as the 'Fighter Mafia' studied the problem and arrived at a solution. It was the 'hi-lo mix', a core of very large and expensive fighters backed by many super-agile lightweights to add quantity to the existing quality.

The accent for the new light fighter was on close combat, with maneuverability, acceleration and endurance stressed, rather than maximum speed and ceiling, the previous goals of fighter design.

General Dynamics (now Lockheed) at Fort Worth, Texas, set up a secure establishment to design the new fighter. In essence they took a large but proven engine and packaged a small airframe, stressed for the then unusual figure of 9*g*, around it. To increase maneuverability it was designed to have 'relaxed stability', and featured wing/body blending and strakes. To save weight, fly-by-wire was used instead of hydraulic control runs (also tested on the F-4 in 1972, inset). Pilot control demands were fed into a computer which automatically translated them into the maximum that the aircraft could take for the speed/altitude combination at the time. Other new features were a steeply raked seat to increase *g* tolerance, and a side-stick controller. The canopy was a one-piece bubble, giving an all-round view. Variable-camber wings provided optimum lift in all flight regimes.

The first flight of the F-16 Fighting Falcon took place on January 20, 1974, with GD test pilot Phil Oestricher at the controls. Later that year it was evaluated against the Northrop F-17, and a year after its first flight it was selected as the new USAF air combat fighter. Within a matter of months it had also been selected by four European air forces.

The F-16 (left) set new standards of agility which became the yardstick by which other fighters were judged for the next two decades. It could sustain a 9*g* turn (albeit over a small portion of the performance envelope) while at the same time establishing a maneuverability plateau close to the limits that a pilot could take.

In the Beka'a action of 1982, to which the opening quotation refers, F-16s accounted for 44 Syrian MiGs for no losses. They also carried out the precision strike against the Osirak nuclear reactor in Iraq in 1981, shot down several Afghan intruders while in Pakistani service, and played a notable part in the Gulf War of 1991.

Right: *The Saab JAS 39 Gripen is a single-seat, single-engined lightweight multi-role fighter which was first flown in December 1988. Problems with the FBW software control laws caused the loss of two aircraft, but these are now thought to have been overcome. Air-to-air weaponry is two Skyflash and four Sidewinder AAMs and a 27mm Mauser BK cannon.*

Below: *The F-16 CCV (Control Configured Vehicle) was developed to explore unconventional flight modes, such as changing altitudes or direction without changing the attitude of the aircraft, by using direct lift or sideforce. Although promising, the concept was never developed.*

Right: *The quest for greater agility has led several manufacturers to adopt the tailless canard delta configuration, coupled with relaxed stability and FBW. The Dassault Rafale is a twin-engined multi-role fighter, the empty weight of which exceeds the normal take-off weight of the Gripen. Production models are the Rafale D (discret=stealth), most of which will be two-seaters, and M (marine), a single-seat carrier fighter. Depicted is the Rafale A prototype.*

Above: *Eurofighter 2000, jointly developed by Britain, Germany, Italy and Spain, is the largest, and potentially most capable but costliest of the European canard deltas. Designed primarily as an air superiority fighter, its agility in combat takes priority and attack capability is secondary. Just test flown in Britain in 1994, up to ten air-to-air missiles can be carried.*

Below: *It has long been known that sweeping the wings forward is in many ways aerodynamically preferable to sweeping them back, but the forces exerted by hard maneuvering would rip them off. Using advanced composites with aero-elastic tailoring gave the necessary strength, and the Grumman X-29 was built to explore this concept.*

Left: *Northrop's YF-17, the unsuccessful contender in the air combat fighter competition, was developed by McDonnell Douglas into the F/A-18 Hornet, seen here in Canadian Armed Forces service. Rather larger than the F-16, the Hornet is an extremely capable multi-role aircraft, able to fly both the agile close-combat fighter and the attack mission.*

Below: *Traditionally, fighter maneuverability has always been restricted by minimum flying speed (Vmin). The ability to maneuver effectively at speeds below Vmin would obviously be a tremendous advantage in close combat, but to date this has not been possible. The Rockwell/MBB X-31A EFM (Enhanced Fighter Maneuverability) demonstrator seen here has been designed with canard foreplanes and thrust-vectoring paddles to explore post-stall maneuverability.*

November 18

STAR WARS COCKPIT

'The E-2 gave us a call, saying "Bandits on nose at 15," which is a confirmed bad guy at 15 [nautical] miles [28km]. We quickly went back to our radar search mode, got locks on them, confirmed they were bad, and shot them both. I fired a Sidewinder at what seemed to be relatively long range, but it wound up working… I fired a Sparrow to make sure. I do believe we're the first guys to kill anybody while carrying 8,000lb (3,629kg) of bombs.'

LT CDR MARK FOX, USN[42]

The above account refers to an incident in the Gulf War when two F/A-18 Hornets, heavily laden for an attack mission against an Iraqi airfield, were intercepted by MiG-21s. At the press of a button or two, Fox and his wingman, Lt Nick 'Mongo' Mongillo, reconfigured their aircraft for air-to-air combat, shot down both of their opponents in a matter of seconds (both of Fox's missiles struck home, Mongillo launched a single Sparrow), then reverted to air-to-ground mode and went on to attack the airfield.

The Hornet (inset) was derived from the Northrop YF-17, developed and navalized by McDonnell Douglas, and first flown on November 18, 1978. The baseline aircraft was intended from the outset to fly both attack and air superiority missions; a different variant for each. But the radar selected, Hughes' APG-65, had multiple modes covering the entire air-to-air and air-to-ground combat spectrum. This allowed a single machine to fly both

missions, the only difference being that two sensor pods would be carried for the attack mission.

The problem then became one of pilot workload. How could one man carry out the multiplicity of tasks efficiently without overloading? Moreover, how could he change quickly from one role to another in flight; from attack to air superiority and back again?

Part of the solution was to hand. McDonnell Douglas had earlier pioneered HOTAS (hands on throttle and stick) in the F-15. This puts every control that the pilot is likely to need during critical phases of flight such as carrier take-offs and landings, or combat, under his hands. It demands extreme manual dexterity, but is far better than having to grope for switches.

Even more importantly, how could the deluge of information available be presented to the pilot in an assimilatable manner? Traditional fighter cockpits were crowded with dials and tape instruments, warning

lights and switches. The situation was not helped by the fact that the Hornet was a small airplane, and panel space was at a premium.

The solution was radical. Basic combat information was presented on the head-up display (HUD) above the panel, while dials and suchlike were almost completely eliminated, being replaced by three small cathode ray tubes (CRTs). Information could be called up on them at the touch of a button.

The CRTs have various functions: radar attack and ground radar mapping, primary warning, armament, infrared sensor information, moving map, attack, navigation, and electronic warfare and threat information. These functions are all interchangeable, and if one CRT fails, either of the others takes over.

The most frequent description used by Hornet pilots is 'like something out of Star Wars.' The F/A-18's cockpit set the trend for all future fighters.

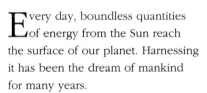

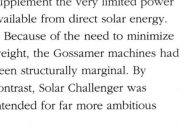

SOLAR CHALLENGER

'What makes the Solar Challenger unique is that it is the first aircraft with sufficient photovoltaic "muscle power" to enable it to fly unaided. Lightweight construction and energy-efficient design have produced the world's first truly solar-powered man-carrying aircraft.'

MARTYN COWLEY[43]

Every day, boundless quantities of energy from the Sun reach the surface of our planet. Harnessing it has been the dream of mankind for many years.

A few flights had been made both in England and the USA using batteries charged by solar energy, but American Dr Paul MacCready set out to design an aircraft capable of powered flight using only energy drawn directly from the Sun's rays.

MacCready was already famous as a designer of successful human-powered aircraft. His Gossamer Condor won the Kremer prize for sustained flight on August 23, 1977, and Gossamer Albatross flew the English Channel on June 12, 1979. He was therefore no stranger to the ultralight construction needed to supplement the very limited power available from direct solar energy.

Because of the need to minimize weight, the Gossamer machines had been structurally marginal. By contrast, Solar Challenger was intended for far more ambitious

flights, and was stressed to +5/-3g. This notwithstanding, its all-up weight, including the pilot, was no more than 294lb (133kg). Probably the most important weight-saving measure was the choice of pilot, Janice Brown, who weighed in at a mere 99lb (45kg).

Solar Challenger was, in effect, a powered glider. A long-span high-set wing was supplemented by a large-area horizontal stabilizer mounted well back on the boom that served as a fuselage. Both surfaces gave plenty of area for the 1,628 solar cells, each about 3/4in x 2/2in x 0.013in (19mm x 63mm x 0.3mm), which provided motive power. An narrow underslung nacelle housed the cockpit, above which the boom projected forward, carrying the electric motor and a variable-pitch propeller. At the extreme rear of the boom was a raked vertical stabilizer and rudder, positioned to minimize the risk of it casting shadows across the cells, with a consequent loss of power.

By November 1980 all was ready for the first flight. Conditions had to be just right. The aircraft had to be facing into wind and aligned with the runway, with the Sun high in the sky and directly astern. On November 20 the team gathered at El Mirage, a gliding center near Shafter, California. The clouds cleared, the Sun shone, and Janice Brown fed power to the electric motor. Solar Challenger rolled gently forward and lifted off. That first flight lasted 2 minutes 50 seconds, in which time a height of 60ft (18m) was achieved.

Other flights followed, an altitude of 14,300ft (4,358m) being reached and endurance being extended to 8 hours 19 minutes. Then, on July 7, 1981, an extensively modified Solar Challenger, piloted by Stephen Ptacek, took off from Cormeilles-en-Vexin near Paris, climbed to 12,000ft (3,657m), crossed the Channel, and landed at Manston in England just 5 hours 25 minutes later. Solar-powered flight was a reality.

December 14-23

VOYAGER

'The autopilot had been acting up again... The ADI was precessing, rolling off, every now and again. Hell, I don't even want to mess with it. I want to eke out every last bit of performance even if it's just an hour or so. We're close enough to home right now that if it quit, we'd probably hand-fly it — which would be one of the most incredible feats that two people would ever have to perform. I'm looking forward to having to hand-fly this airplane like I'd look at the electric chair...'

DICK RUTAN [44]

Voyager, designed by Burt Rutan to fly around the world non-stop and unrefueled, was a very unconventional aeroplane.

The best description of Voyager is a trimaran with wings. This layout was adopted to combine maximum fuel capacity with minimum necessary cruising power and drag. A small piston engine was mounted at each end of a central nacelle; two engines were needed for take-off and climb, and flight at high weights. Later, when sufficient fuel had been burned off, the front engine could be shut down. Between the engines was a cramped cockpit and a barely adequate sleeping area.

Outboard of the nacelle were two long booms, with vertical tail surfaces mounted on them. The booms were almost entirely filled with fuel, although a small weather radar was mounted on the nose of the right one.

The booms were connected to the nacelle by a canard surface at the nose and by the wing at the halfway point. The wing itself was a tour-de-force; optimised for high lift and low drag, it was very long and narrow, with winglets at its extremities. It also housed fuel. Construction was of lightweight composite materials.

Planning the flight and building the aircraft occupied several years, but finally all was ready. Voyager was piloted by Dick Rutan, brother of the designer, and Jeana Yeager.

Edwards AFB, in the Mojave desert, boasts the world's longest runway, 15,000ft (4.57km). It was here that Voyager took off on its epic flight on the morning of December 14, 1986. Disaster seemed imminent at the start. Laden with 996 gal (1,200 US gal) of fuel, Voyager took 14,000ft (4.27km) of runway to become airborne, the winglets scraping the ground and breaking off. Undaunted, the Voyager crew gained height and turned west, toward the Pacific. They were on their way.

The flight was not easy. Severe turbulence could cause Voyager to break up, so it had to be detected and avoided. The autopilot needed constant adjustment to suit changing flight conditions; fuel had to be correctly balanced, and navigation monitored.

Hours turned into days as Voyager travelled steadily westwards. Beyond the Pacific, over Thailand, Sri Lanka, the shark-infested Indian Ocean; on over the continent of Africa.

Various mechanical problems arose, but fatigue was the real enemy. The autopilot gave trouble, as did one or two instruments, but Voyager flew on, across the South Atlantic to South America, across Panama, then up the west coast of the USA and finally back to Edwards, touching down after 9 days 3 minutes and 44 seconds. A distance of 24,986 statute miles (40,209km) had been covered, and just 31 gal (37 US gal) of fuel remained. It had been a close-run thing indeed.

February 22

FBW AIRLINER

'Our A320 behaved even better than expected— it is both delightfully responsive and reassuringly stable to fly, qualities which fly-by-wire brings together for the first time in an airliner. Never before have we enjoyed a first flight so much, and we are confident that airline pilots will feel the same way.'

PIERRE BAUD[45]

The Airbus A320 is a short-to-medium-range twin-engined commercial transport developed from the earlier A300 series. Externally there is little to distinguish it from the many other shorthaul airliners in service around the world, but under the skin it is very different.

The A320 features a number of airliner 'firsts,' including a centralized maintenance system, gust alleviation and the extensive use of composite materials in its primary structure. Most significantly, it is the first subsonic commercial aircraft to be fitted with a fly-by-wire flight control system (FCS).

Instead of the conventional control column, the pilot and copilot each have a side-stick control similar to that pioneered in the General Dynamics F-16 fighter. Pitch and roll commands are signalled to a bank of five computers, which in turn pass them to the hydraulically operated flight control surfaces. A very high degree of protection is built in. The system will not allow structural and aerodynamic limits such as design speed or *g* to be exceeded, while a full nose-up command will give maximum lift and no more. The aircraft will hang on the edge of the flight performance envelope without ever straying outside it. This means that the A320 cannot be stalled or overstressed while in the automatic mode, and is thus potentially the safest aircraft in service anywhere.

As a further safety measure, the automatic FCS can be turned off and the aircraft flown manually, while backup control is provided by a conventional mechanical system to the rudder and horizontal stabilizer trimmers.

A visit to the flight deck is instructive. Whereas, on older aircraft, the instrument panel was smothered with dials and other instruments, that of the A320 is remarkably free of clutter. It is dominated by a series of electronic flight instrumentation systems (EFIS), on which is shown (in color) all essential flight and navigation information (inset). Another first here is that the primary flight display incorporates speed, altitude and heading. Other displays show continually monitored engine performance, warnings, and system diagrams.

Further remarkable facts about the Airbus A320 are that it is the product of 100% computer aided design (CAD) and 80% computer-assisted manufacture (CAM). The first flight was made from Toulouse on February 22, 1987, and the first deliveries, to Air France and British Caledonian (now part of BA), were made late in March 1988.

The A320 was originally built as the -100, but this was soon superseded by the -200, which has wingtip winglets, a greater maximum take-off weight, and increased range. As at May 31, 1993, firm orders totalled 657, with 400 delivered. In all, 397 are in service with more than 25 airlines.

HAVE BLUE

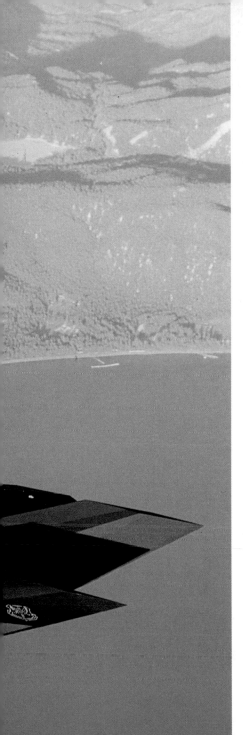

November 10

STEALTH REVEALED

'Being a stealth pilot is one of the most labor intensive and time constrained types of flying that I know. We have very strict timing constraints: to be where you are supposed to be all the time, exactly on time, and that has to be monitored by the pilot. For example, during a bomb competition in training in the US, I dropped a weapon that landed 0.02 seconds from the desired time, and finished third!'

LT COL MILES POUND, USAF [46]

In the 'Invisible Man' films, the hero is able to carry out tasks that would otherwise have been impossible, because no-one can see him to stop him. The 'Invisible Man' of the aviation world is the Lockheed F-117A.

It is, of course, impossible to build an invisible aircraft, but steps can be taken along the road. Ever since the Second World War, radar has assumed an increasingly dominant role, firstly in the field of detection, and secondly as a means of missile guidance and gun-laying. This being the case, electronic invisibility became a sought-after attribute.

There are two basic ways to lower the radar 'signature' of an aircraft. Building it from radar-absorbent materials (RAM) is one; the other is to shape the aircraft in such a way that electronic emissions are deflected away from the receiver instead of back to it. The former method was simple; the latter was very difficult.

Various steps were taken from the 1950s onwards, but a truly low observable penetrator seemed a long way in the future.

The computers of the 1970s were not advanced enough to predict the radar cross-section (RCS) of curved surfaces with sufficient accuracy. What could be done, however, was to design an aircraft as a series of flat plates at angles calculated to deflect instead of reflect radar emissions.

This posed another problem. Conventional aerodynamics simply would not apply. The angular shape would have impossible flying characteristics, with excessive drag. By now technology was catching up. The F-16 had a digital fly-by-wire system and this, combined with suitable software, was used to tame the oddly-shaped airframe. Extreme measures were also taken to minimize the aeroplane's infrared signature. The theory could only be proven in the air, and two scaled-down proof-of-concept machines

were built (inset). Trials flown in 1977-78 gave promising results.

The next step was to build the full-size machine, the Lockheed F-117A, and the first flight took place on June 18, 1981. Difficulties were encountered in the development phase. Test pilot Tom Morgenfeld recalled, 'It did everything but sit on its tail while it was standing on its wheels!', but finally the airplane was tamed.

Under conditions of absolute secrecy the F-117A was brought into operational service. All training missions were flown by night. This was hardly surprising; the Black Jet was too vulnerable to operate in daylight, where fighters might encounter it visually. Not until November 10, 1988, was its existence revealed. After a less-than-impressive combat debut over Panama, the Black Jet proved its worth in the Gulf War of 1991, repeatedly penetrating the Iraqi air defenses undetected and making precision attacks on selected targets.

Left: *F-117A pilots are seated at the center of an information explosion, reliant on extremely precise flying and navigation to find and attack their targets, as to maintain low observability, they cannot use detectable aids which are emitters, such as radar ground mapping.*

Below: *Two Black Jets exude menace as they sit at dispersal. The faceted shape, designed to deflect radar returns away from the emitter, and the carefully shielded engine intakes, are seen to advantage from this angle. The completely flat underside does of course reflect radar, but only when the F-117A is almost exactly overhead, which is a blind spot for almost all ground radars.*

Right: *Advances in computer technology enabled the radar cross-section of curved surfaces to be calculated to a reasonable degree of accuracy. The next generation stealth aircraft was the Northorp B-2 Spirit seen here, which combined straight leading and trailing edges with smoothly contoured curves to give an aerodynamic shape. Note that the engine effluxes are shielded.*

Right, below: *A view of the front of an F-117A from vertically above. As can be seen, even air data sensor probes are faceted, while the radar shielding to the port inlet shows up well. The view forward and down from the cockpit, penalized by stealth requirements, is obviously poor.*

GARGANTUAN

'I arrived over Le Bourget with Buran (the Russian space shuttle) on the back of my aircraft. The clouds were low, and there was drizzle. Visibility was poor, and I had to fly a steep turn beneath the clouds to line up with the runway before landing. It was no problem; I was flying with one hand only! Then to show that this aeroplane can go anywhere, after landing I taxied across the grass to the parking place.'

ANATOLI BULANENKO[47]

These few words by the pilot of the Antonov An-225 summarize a remarkable demonstration of the low-speed control and agility, and rough field performance, of the world's largest aircraft, and the pilot's confidence in his machine. It all sounds so easy, but in fact the circuit, made in poor visibility at what seemed barely one wingspan height above the ground, followed by a turn off the taxiway and across the soggy grass surface, impressed even the hardened aviation journalists present. The Russian space shuttle carried piggyback on the monster aircraft simply added to the effect.

The An-225 is a heavy transport designed to carry enormous loads internally or outsize loads externally. It is the biggest and heaviest aircraft ever to fly. Its overall length is 275ft (84m); the maximum take-off weight is 590 tons (600 tonnes) and maximum payload is 246 tons (250 tonnes). The engines are six Lotarev D-18T turbofans, each providing

51,590lb (229.5kN) of thrust, and range with a 197-ton (200-tonne) payload is 2,425 n.m. (4,500km).

The An-225 was developed from what was previously the world's largest aircraft, the An-124. The fuselage was stretched, the rear loading doors deleted, and a new wing center section, two more turbofans and a completely new twin-fin tail unit introduced. Named Mriya (Dream), the An-225 made its maiden flight on December 21, 1988. Within four months it had set 106 world and class records. Then in June 1989 it made its first public appearance in the West, carrying, for greater effect, the Russian space shuttle *Buran* (main picture).

Russia was a pioneer in the field of very large aircraft. The first four-engined airplane to fly was Igor Sikorsky's *Le Grand*, on May 26, 1913, at St Petersburg. This was developed into the Il'ya Muromets, (inset) the first four-engined bomber.

After the revolution, the design of large aircraft continued. The first of

these, in December 1930, was the four-engined TB-3 bomber, followed three years later by the six-engined TB-4, at that time the world's largest aircraft. The ANT-20 *Maxim Gorkii* was an eight-engined behemoth first shown to the public on May 19, 1934. Essentially a propaganda exercise, this was equipped with a cinema, a printing press and a broadcasting studio, and carried a crew of 20 and 50 passengers. The exercise turned sour a year later when it crashed after a mid-air collision.

Even bigger aircraft were planned, the 12-engined TB-6 among them, but the wish had outrun the technology. The final prewar design to enter service was the TB-7 (Pe-8).

The quest for sheer size lapsed until 1957, with the debut of the Tu-114, at that time the largest commercial aircraft in the world. In 1965 the huge An-22 Anteus transport made its appearance, followed by the An-124 Ruslan in 1982. But biggest of all is Mriya.

September 29

ULTIMATE FIGHTER

'With the Lockheed fighter, a US pilot can enter any part of the spectrum of aerial combat against numerous contenders, with the confidence that he has the top fighter strapped to his butt. This bird of prey will kill and maim anything the enemy can get airborne and our guy will return home safely and victoriously. This is the embodiment of combat confidence.'

GEN FRED HAEFFNER, USAF (RET) [48]

The man who wrote those words is no stranger to air combat. On May 13, 1967, Lt Col Fred Haeffner was flying an F-4C with the 8th TFW in Vietnam, the famous Wolf Pack. Leaving the Yen Vien area after providing cover for a strike, he saw MiG-17s chasing F-105s. Diving on the North Vietnamese fighters, he launched three AIM-7 Sparrows in quick succession. The first missed by about 100ft (30m), but the second impacted just aft of the cockpit, destroying the MiG-17.

The new fighter about which Gen Haeffner was waxing lyrical is the Lockheed F-22, selected as the USAF air-superiority fighter of the future. What makes it special?

The Lightning II, as it is now named, is the result of a totally new approach to air combat, utilizing stealth and speed as never before.

The essential thing is to detect without being detected, as this gives the initiative. The F-22 combines state-of-the-art low observables, which make it hard to detect, with the latest detection sensors. All else being equal, it will therefore have both the initiative and the first shot.

Externally, the F-22 is clean and uncluttered. To minimize RCS all fuel is carried internally, as are the air-to-air missiles, which are housed in bays. It is the first US fighter to carry weapons internally since the F-106.

Speed is the other factor. Many aircraft can attain high speeds by using afterburner, but they cannot sustain them without running out of fuel. The Lightning II is designed to supercruise (to cruise at supersonic speed, Mach 1.4 or more) using military power only, which means that it can supercruise for extended periods. Supercruise has other enormous advantages. Even if an opponent manages to detect the Lightning II, it will be very hard-pressed to reach an attacking position in the time available, and converting to the traditional astern attack position is nearly impossible. Another factor is that high speed restricts missile launch envelopes to a tremendous degree; an attacker will have to get very close to bring his missiles within range. Mach 1.4 is widely regarded as the speed which keeps a fighter's tail clear under most circumstances, and it is probable that the F-22 can supercruise at speeds significantly greater than this.

Even if close maneuver combat is joined (and the combination of speed and stealth make this unlikely unless the F-22 pilot wishes it), the Lockheed fighter, which is fitted with vectoring nozzles, lacks nothing in maneuverability, and carries a gun for really close work. Handling is described as excellent; 'you only have to think it and you find yourself doing it.'

Although designed as the ultimate fighter, the latest tactical thinking seems to indicate that air-to-surface ordnance will also be carried.

Out of missiles? Disengagement? Supercruise and stealth make it easy. The F-22 has no weak points.

SOURCE NOTES

1 Orville Wright's telegraph in Kelly, New York, 1966.
2 Orville Wright in *Boys Life* magazine, September 1914, USA.
3 Orville Wright in *Boys Life* magazine, September 1914, USA.
4 Emile Berliner in Gregory, London, 1948.
5 Louis Bleriot in Mackworth-Praed (ed.), London, 1990.
6 Louis Bleriot in Mackworth-Praed (ed.), London, 1990.
7 Capt Chambers in Turnbull, Yale, 1949.
8 McCudden, London, 1939.
9 Sir Arthur Whitten Brown in Alcock and Brown, London, 1969.
10 Gregory, London, 1948.
11 Bill Sherer in Douglas S. Ritter, 'Gas Stations in the Sky' in *Code One*, Fort Worth, January 1993.
12 Leslie Arnold in Claudia M. Oakes, Washington, 1981.
13 Lindbergh, New York, 1952.
14 Wiley Post in Post and Gatty, London, 1932.
15 L.V. Stewart Blacker in *The Times*, London, April 4, 1933.
16 Erich Hartmann in Cunningham et al, Fort Worth, 1990.
17 James W. Johnson in Freeman, London, 1977.
18 Alec Blythe in Arthur, London, 1993.
19 Reitsch, London, 1955.
20 Galland, London, 1955.
21 Braham, London, 1961.
22 Lamb, London, 1977.
23 Cheshire, London, 1943.
24 Rupert Clark in Price, London, 1993.
25 George Caron in Thomas and Witts, London, 1977.
26 Harbison, 1953.
27 Charles 'Chuck' Yeager in Yeager and Janos, London, 1986.
28 Anthony Cecchini in Rodrigo, London, 1960.
29 Harvey, London, 1958.
30 Sharp, Shrewsbury 1960.
31 Carl Gramlick in Bin and Hill, unpublished manuscript.
32 Broughton, New York, 1988.
33 Broughton, New York, 1988.
34 Scott Crossfield, 'My Flights Towards Space' in *RAF Flying Review*, London, August 1960.
35 Dunn, Iowa, 1986.
36 Don Walbrecht in Crickmore, London, 1993.
37 Terryl Morris in Chinnery, London, 1988.
38 Tom Miller interviewed in BBC documentary 'Jump Jet' in 1985.
39 Paul Wagner, 'First Flight' in *Boeing Magazine*, Seattle, March, 1969.
40 Orlebar, London, 1986.
41 Pilot quoted in Halperin and Lapidot, London, 1990.
42 Mark Fox quoted in Downey in *War Stories*, St Louis, May 13, 1991.
43 Martyn Cowley, 'Wings in the Sun, the Evolution of Solar Challenger' in *Flight International*, London, June 13, 1981.
44 Dick Rutan in Yeager and Rutan, London, 1987.
45 Pierre Baud in *Airbus News* (press release), February 22, 1987.
46 Miles Pound in Bin and Hill, unpublished manuscript.
47 Anatoli Bulanenko in conversation with journalists at Le Bourget, Paris, June 1989.
48 Fred Haeffner in Thomas J. Goff, 'Sherm Mullin: Pushing the Envelope' in *Lockheed Air Power*, December 1990.

BIBLIOGRAPHY

The following is a list of sources consulted by the author in the preparation of this work. Those available to the public are recommended for further reading.

BOOKS

Alcock, Sir John, and Brown, Sir Arthur Whitten, *Our Transatlantic Flight* William Kimber, London, 1969.

Alexander, Jean, *Russian Aircraft Since 1940* Putnam, London, 1975.

Anderton, David A., *Strategic Air Command* Ian Allan, London 1975.

Arthur, Max, *There Shall Be Wings; The RAF from 1918 to the Present* Hodder & Stoughton, London, 1993.

Barker, Ralph, *The Thousand Plan* Chatto & Windus, London, 1965.

Barron, John, *MiG Pilot* Avon Books, New York, 1980.

Bin, Alberto and Hill, Richard. *War, Politics and the Media, Desert Storm 1991* Unpublished manuscript.

Boyne, Walter J. ed., *The Smithsonian Book of Flight* Sidgewick & Jackson, London, 1987.

Braham, Wg Cdr J.R.D. *Scramble* Frederick Muller, London, 1961.

Broughton, Jack, *Thud Ridge* Bantam Books, New York, 1985.

Broughton, Jack, *Going Downtown, the War against Hanoi and Washington* Orion Books, New York, 1988.

Brown, David; Shores, Christopher; and Macksey, Kenneth, *The Guinness History of Air Warfare* Guinness Superlatives, London, 1976.

Campbell, Christopher, *Aces and Aircraft of World War I* Blandford Press, London, 1981.

Cheshire, Gp Capt Leonard, VC, *Bomber Pilot.* Hutchinson, London 1943.

Chinnery, Philip D., *Life on the Line, Stories of Vietnam Air Combat* Blandford Press, London, 1988.

Crickmore, Paul, *Lockheed SR-71, The Secret Missions Exposed* Osprey, London, 1993.

Cunningham, Bob; Simons, Bob; McKinney, Jim; and Smith, Robert, *Tumult in the Clouds* General Dynamics, Forth Worth, 1990.

Dunn, Maj Peter M., *Flying Combat Aircraft of the USAAF/USAF* Iowa State University Press, 1986

Freeman, Roger, *B-17 Fortress at War* Ian Allan, London, 1977.

Futrell, R. Frank, et al, *Aces and Aerial Victories, The United States Air Force in Southeast Asia 1965–1973* The Albert F. Simpson Historical Research Center, Air University, and Office of Air Force History HQ, Washington DC, 1976.

Galland, Adolf, *The First and the Last* Methuen, London, 1955.

Green, William, *Famous Bombers of the Second World War* Macdonald & Jane's, London, 1975.

Green, William, *Famous Fighters of the Second World War* Macdonald & Jane's, London, 1975.

Gregory, Col H.F., *The Helicopter, or Anything a Horse can do* George Allen & Unwin. London, 1948.

Gunston, Bill, ed., *Chronicle of Aviation* Chronicle Communications Ltd., London, 1992.

Gunston, Bill, *General Dynamics F-111* Ian Allan, London, 1978.

Gunston, Bill and Spick, Mike, *Modern Fighting Helicopters* Salamander Books, London, 1986.

Gunston, Bill, *Night Fighters, A Development and Combat History* Patrick Stephens, Cambridge, 1976.

Halperin, Merav and Lapidot, Aharon, *G-Suit: Combat Reports from Israel's Air War* Sphere Books, London, 1990.

Harvey, Derek, *The Viscount* Cassell, London, 1958.

Harvey, Derek, *The Comet* Cassell, London, 1959.

James, Derek N., *Westland Aircraft Since 1915* Putnam, London, 1991.

Jane's All the World's Aircraft various years.

Kelly, Fred C., *The Wright Brothers* New York, 1966.

Lamb, Cdr Charles, *War in a Stringbag* Cassell, London, 1977.

Lindbergh, Charles A., *The Spirit of St Louis* New York, 1952.

Mackworth-Praed, Ben, ed., *Aviation, the Pioneer Years* Studio Editions, London 1990.

McCudden, James, VC, *Flying Fury* The Aviation Book Club, London, 1939.

Miller, Jay, *Lockheed F-117 Stealth Fighter* Aerofax. Arlington, Texas, 1992.

Mondey, David, *Westland* Jane's, London, 1982.

Nemecek, Vaclav, *The History of Soviet Aircraft from 1918* Willow Books, London, 1986.

Oakes, Claudia M. comp., *Aircraft of the National Air and Space Museum* Smithsonian Institution, Washington DC, 1981.

Orlebar, Christopher, *The Concorde Story* Temple Press, London, 1986.

Pearcy, Arthur, *Fifty Glorious Years* Airlife Publishing, Shrewsbury, 1985.

Post, Wiley, and Gatty, Harold, *Around the World in Eight Days* John Hamilton, London, 1932.

Price, Alfred, *Blitz on Britain 1939-1945* Ian Allan, London, 1977.

Price, Alfred, *Sky Battles; Dramatic Air Warfare Actions* Arms & Armour, London, 1993.

Redding, Robert, and Yenne, Bill, *Boeing, Planemaker to the World* Arms & Armour, London, 1983.

Reitsch, Hanna, *The Sky My Kingdom* Bodley Head, London, 1955.

Richardson, Doug, *F-16 Fact File* Salamander Books, London, 1983.

Rodrigo, Robert, *Berlin Airlift* Cassell, London 1960.

Sharp, C. Martin, *DH, A History of de Havilland* Airlife Publishing, Shrewsbury, 1960.

Smith, J.R., and Kay, Antony, *German Aircraft of the Second World War* Putnam, London, 1972.

Spick, Mike, *The Ace Factor, Air Combat and the Role of Situational Awareness* Airlife Publishing, Shrewsbury, 1988.

Spick, Mike, *All-Weather Warriors, Arms & Armour Press* London, 1994.

Spick, Mike, *American Spyplanes* Osprey, London, 1986.

Spick, Mike, *BAe/McDD Harrier* Salamander Books, London, 1991.

Spick, Mike, *F/A-18 Fact File* Salamander Books, London, 1984.

Spick, Mike, *Fighter Pilot Tactics* Patrick Stephens, Cambridge, 1983.

Spick, Mike, *Jet Fighter Performance, Korea to Vietnam* Ian Allan, London, 1986.

Taylor, John W.R., *A History of Aerial Warfare* Hamlyn, London, 1974.

Taylor, John W.R., ed, compiled by H.F. King, *Jane's 100 Significant Aircraft 1909–1969*, London, 1970.

Taylor, Michael, and Mondey, David, ed., *The Guinness Book of Aircraft Facts and Feats* Guinness Superlatives, London, 1984.

These Tremendous Years, 1919–1938, Daily Express, London, 1938.

Thetford, Owen, *Aircraft of the Royal Air Force since 1918* Putnam, London, 1976.

Thomas, Gordon, and Witts, Max Morgan, *Ruin from the Air, the Atomic Mission to Hiroshima* Hamish Hamilton, London, 1977.

Turnbull, A.D., *History of United States Naval Aviation* Yale University Press, 1949.

Werner, Johannes, *Knight of Germany* John Hamilton, London, 1933.

Wheeler, Howard A., *Attack Helicopters, a History of Rotary-Wing Combat Aircraft* Greenhill Books, London, 1987.

Winchester, Clarence, ed., *Wonders of World Aviation* Amalgamated Press, London, 1938.

Winton, John, *Air Power at Sea 1939–45* Sidgewick & Jackson, London, 1976.

Wragg, David, *Airlift, a History of Military Air Transport* Airlife Publishing, Shrewsbury, 1986.

Yeager, General Chuck, and Janos, Leo, *Yeager* Century Hutchinson, London, 1986.

Yeager, Jeanna, and Rutan, Dick *Voyager* Heinemann, London, 1987.

MAGAZINES

Aeroplane Monthly, Aug 1981.

Aerospace, Journal of the Royal Aeronautical Society, Nov. 1992, Dec. 1993.

Air Enthusiast Nos. 6 and 41.
AirForces Monthly, June 1991, Jan 1994.
Air International, March/April/May 1975, Jan 1986, Sept 1986, Oct 1986, Mar 1989, May 1989, Sept 1990, Jan 1994.
Boeing Magazine, March 1969.
Boys Life, Sept 1914.
Code One, Lockheed Fort Worth Division House Magazine, Jan 1993.
Flight International, 13 June 1981.
Flight International Show Daily, 14 June 1989

(le Bourget), 4 September 1990 (Farnborough).
Flypast, May 1991, May 1992.
Horizons, Grumman House Magazine, 1985.
Lockheed Air Power, House Magazine, December 1990.
Naval Aviation News, 75th Anniversary Edn, May 1986.
Naval Aviation News, Special Edition, 1984.
RAF Flying Review, various issues.
Rolls-Royce Magazine, Sept-Nov 1980.
Saturday Evening Post (undated)
The Times, Tuesday 4 April 1933.
War Stories, McDonnell Douglas, 13 May 1991.

OTHER SOURCES

F/A-18 Hornet Crew Station. Undated paper by Eugene C. Adam, McDonnell Aircraft Company.
Fighter Versus Fighter Operations in Korea. RAF Central Fighter Establishment paper by Sqn Ldr Paddy Harbison, 1953.
Variable Sweep Wing Design. Paper presented to AIAA Conference by Robert W. Kress, Director of Advanced Concepts, Grumman, March 1980.
Jump Jet, BBC TV Documentary, 1985.
Airbus Industrie, various press releases.

PICTURE CREDITS